SHARING THE SEARCH

Sharing the Search

*A THEOLOGY
OF CHRISTIAN
HOSPITALITY*

THOMAS R. HAWKINS

The Upper Room
Nashville, Tennessee

Sharing the Search

Cover Design: Roy Wallace
First Printing: April 1988 (7)
Library of Congress Catalog Card Number: 87-051424
ISBN: 0-8358-0583-2

Printed in the United States of America.

In Memory Of

Dolly Wiseman Jewel

She is generous to the poor and needy.
Give her credit for all she does. She de-
serves the respect of everyone.
—Proverbs 31:20, 31 TEV

CONTENTS

___

ONE

   We Need More than Bread and Water—We Need Each Other   11

TWO

   We Are Our Brothers' and Sisters' Keepers   27

THREE

   Jesus Came to Eat and Drink with Sinners   47

FOUR

   Hospitality—Catalyst for Partnerships in the Gospel   69

FIVE

   Spirit of the Living God, Fall Afresh on Us   89

SIX

   Pilgrimage into the Strange Absence of God in Public Life   105

SHARING THE SEARCH

ONE

We Need More than Bread and Water
—We Need Each Other

The envelope's solitary note read, "When we cleaned out Mom and Dad's house, we found all these pictures. Since some of them were of you and your family, we thought you might like them." I sat in the rocker, looking out at the scrub oaks and the seashore in the background, and sorted through the random collection of photographs taken across more than twenty years of my family's life together.

They came, however, at just the wrong moment in my life. It was a time when I felt particularly isolated and adrift, when I was in transition in my life. Everything felt tentative, temporary. I was terminating a pastoral relationship. A marriage of some ten years seemed to have finally and completely unraveled. The isolation and loneliness of Cape Cod, cut off from the mainland by a broad and deep canal, only served to deepen my sense of being cut off, of being at sea. I asked myself, "Who am I?" No answer easily came to mind. In fact, I felt as if I could have been any one of several selves. Some days I would awaken with a start and not know for sure who I was. Other days I would be in a group of co-workers or friends where I had a sure and certain sense of myself. And yet just hours later I would not be able to connect this self with how I was responding and feeling at that moment.

So I sat in the late afternoon sunlight, thumbing through a pile of fading color prints and glossy black and white photographs and looking at a world with which I could no longer identify. Yes, these were familiar rooms I saw. Yes, these were people I had known. And yet, I could not visualize myself within this world. I stared blankly into the frozen images of my childhood, but I could not find myself there. Somehow, I knew that little boy was me, sitting there beside a half-dozen cousins under the Christmas tree. But any invisible umbilical cord that tied me to that six-year-old boy had long been cut. Yes, that was me politely tucked up against the dining room table while the Thanksgiving turkey and all the trimmings were scattered along the board. But that young child and I were strangers to each other. If we had once met and shared a common moment in time, that moment had forged no bonds and left no lasting connection.

I stood up. I shuffled through the photos one more time and pulled out a number of school pictures that my aunt and uncle must have saved. Had I given these to them? Had I proudly presented them with the bill-fold-sized school picture some Sunday afternoon as we ate homemade ice cream and angel food cake? On the floor I arranged all these pictures of me in some vaguely chronological order. Was this me? The eyeglasses changed from year to year, casualties of one accident after another on the playground. The shirts were different.

I could remember the eyeglasses and the shirts more clearly than the face I saw frowning into the camera's eye. Was that really me? Could that be me? Perhaps we take so many photographs, carefully paste them into albums, and carry them with us because we hope that, somehow, the sequence of photographs will tell us where we have been and, consequently, who we are. The flat frozen image in the faded photo serves as a substitute for the lifelong living relationships that inform us and confirm our essential identity. But these photographs could not even do that for me. They only deepened my sense of loss and confusion.

Strangely, however, the photos came as both judgment and grace into my life. They came as judgment because, as I sat there that afternoon, choked with emotion and aching with a sense of a world I had lost and could never regain, I realized what had gone amiss in my life. They came as grace because, in that moment of judgment, I realized that there was a ground for hope, a means to rebuild my life and to recover a sense of myself.

Until that afternoon, I had been living under the illusion that I could forge my own identity. I had thought that the self was a product each of us could create out of our own choices, options, and actions. I had thought that my own identity was something self-contained, that I could somehow choose who I would be, that my life was a self-creation. This illusion had led me into hopeless competition with myself. This was why I no longer could recognize myself in the old photographs: I had set myself in competition not only with others but with myself. "That we can forge our own identities; that we are the collective impressions of our surroundings; that we are the trophies and distinctions we have won. This, indeed, is our greatest illusion. It makes us into competitive people who compulsively cling to our differences and defend them at all cost, even to the point of violence."[1]

I should have known this. The whole of the biblical tradition announces over and over again that our identity comes as gift and not as self-created product. Our identity comes as grace. I should have known this—I had heard it often enough. I had even said it frequently to others as well as to myself. Yet I had never really heard it. I had never truly understood it until that afternoon, as the old photographs lay about me like so many dry and crumbling leaves.

I had never really paused to consider the way in which God's grace operates within our lives. I had assumed that grace was purely a private matter between me and my God. All that mattered was some assurance of the heart that was mediated directly between my heart and God's heart. I had understood the inward journey as one that involved only my inner self and God. Such a preoccupation had blinded me. It had focused me so intensely upon my inner self that I had ignored all the other ways in which God spoke to me, reached out to me, shaped my selfhood. My understanding of God's means of grace in my life was insufficient.

Just pay attention to the inner voice, the inner light, I had thought, *and you will discover who you are.* My individualistic attention to this inner voice had turned me in upon myself in such a way that I had lost my bearings. In Hebrew, the personal pronoun *I* begins with the consonant *aleph*. By itself, according to the Jewish midrash upon the Hebrew alphabet's symbolic meaning, *aleph* is silent. It is without sound. It therefore depends upon the surrounding vowels and consonants to give it meaning. So it is with us, the midrash continues; alone we are unreal. Our lives are silent. Our lives can speak and our selfhood reveals itself only when we are linked to surrounding lives.

Early Israel could not conceive of the individual self apart from social processes and relationships. Genesis's fundamental affirmations about human existence include the belief that men and women exist as true selves only through their mutuality, through their being in relationship to one another. "It is not good that Adam should be alone," states God (Gen. 2:18, AP). Throughout Israel's history, dispersion among the nations is a curse. To live an isolated life not bound together with other lives within a community is the final curse. It is a sign of death. Reunion, being gathered together from among the nations, is conversely a sign of blessing. "For the Bible, to be dispersed into solitude is to know the deathly terror of nothingness. To be alone, ultimately alone, is to be desolate, deprived of everything that makes life human."[2]

> Behold, how good and pleasant it is
> when brothers and sisters dwell in unity!
> It is like the precious oil upon the head,
> running down upon the beard,
> upon the beard of Aaron
>
> . . . .
>
> For there the Lord has commanded the blessing,
> life for evermore.
> —Psalm 133:1-2, 3

Contrary to this understanding, I had believed that the arena of my inner life was purely a private matter. After all, had I not been taught that the spiritual life is the "interior" life? Such individualistic assumptions, of course, caused me to turn in upon myself. Eventually, I became entangled in the many selves I spun for myself, none of whom helped me clarify my true identity before God. I had thought that I had within me some special gift, some structure of selfhood uniquely mine, and that it was my task to uncover and to live according to it.

Such an understanding of the spiritual life, however, is based more closely upon ancient Greek models than biblical ones. According to James Fowler in *Becoming Adult, Becoming Christian*, pre-hellenic Greek sculptors made busts of the semi-deity Silenus that had a trick to them. Inside the hollow clay statue a golden figurine was hidden, a figurine that could be revealed only when the clay statue was broken open.[3] This bust and its hidden figurine symbolized the human task of what contemporary psychology calls "self-actualization": We break open the crust of our socially constructed masks and discover the golden figurine of our true selves. Our single passion in life under this system becomes the realization of our unique and special excellence.

Such an understanding of the spiritual life, however, is flawed by a major misconception: the individualistic assumption that we are or can be completely selfgrounded persons. Secular versions of this heresy assume that we have within us—or can generate within us—all the resources needed to live a fulfilled, selfactualized life. Some Christian versions of this perspective imply that God has buried these resources deep within us, that the tangled relationships we have with others in social life have caused us to bury or distort this true self. Our task, then, is to peel away the social masks and recover our God-given selfhood, a process somehow understood as a purely private journey. We and God alone can do this.

A few questions undermine this understanding: What if the social relationships that have shaped and continue to shape our lives are not merely sources of distortion and causes of the formation of a false self? What if, instead, it is through such social means that God intends for the true self to take shape? These means may sometimes lead to distortion and perversion of our selfhood; they may sometimes be a source of our falsity and self-deception. But they may be a primary means of correcting such falsity as well.

Perhaps the old doctrine of prevenient grace, a doctrine especially important to John and Charles Wesley, comes into play here: God goes before us, shaping our lives and gifting us with our identity through our social existence. Abbé Huvelin wrote, "God who might have created us directly, employs for this work, our parents, to whom He joins us by the tenderest ties. He could also save us directly, but he saves us, in fact, by means of certain souls, which have received the spiritual life before ourselves, and which communicate it to us, because they love us."[4]

A few years ago *The New Yorker* carried an article that told of the search for Sam Todd. Todd, a Yale Divinity School student, disappeared after a New Year's Eve party on Mulberry Street in Greenwich Village. In the weeks after his disappearance, his family and friends staged a citywide hunt for him. His parents and brothers dropped their work to open an office in a Greenwich Village church; over two hundred classmates and friends came to New York City to search for him. In commenting on this sad, noble, but fruitless search, *The New Yorker* author observed:

> The wide sea that seems to separate most of us from the derelicts and the dirty street people and the homeless is really about as broad as the Harlem River up at 145th Street, where a good heave will land a rock safely in the Bronx. . . . In purely practical terms, our lives are not nearly so far away as most of us imagine from those of the men with the matted beards who wander through

Astor Place, those of the eternally tired women with their Shopwell plastic bags. It is the rare person who could not conceivably be reduced to the same raggedy shape by a combination of plausible circumstances—the loss of a job, the breakup of a marriage, an encounter with alcoholism, a bout of mental illness, a sudden disability. For most of us, misfortunes like these are mere catastrophes; for some people, such events are enough to turn them into the ghosts who wander the city wrapped in blankets, enough to make them think of the Port Authority bus station as home. . . . One reason for the different outcomes—maybe the main reason—is that most of us, when we fall, are saved by people who care enough to catch us, and who have the strength.[5]

The single most important difference, then, is that some of us have social networks strong enough to catch us when we fall. What does the ideology of individual self-actualization have to say about the less fortunate victims of life? There seems to be no golden figure within the clay statue for these broken men and women. If we are all truly self-grounded, then these people should have the resources they need within. If they cannot cope with life, are they themselves to blame?

Perhaps, however, Huvelin is correct and our resources come to us from beyond our lives. They come quietly into our lives through the social relationships, the mutuality and sociality that constitute the fabric of our lives. Perhaps such sociality and mutuality are in fact the means of God's prevenient grace. It is not enough for Adam to be placed alone in the world. Adam is not self-grounded. The gift of mutuality and human relationship through Eve is necessary for truly human existence.

Our identities are not hidden within us, to be discovered in a purely interior, individual journey. Instead, our identities are given to us through the daily give-and-take of human relationships. While it is true that such social exchanges can encourage us to develop distorted masks that constrict and bury our genuine selfhood, such sociality can also be a means of grace. And like all means of grace it can be distorted and misused. As imperfect as it may be, without social mutuality we are deprived of the resources to construct any genuine sense of who we are before God.

Exclusion from meaningful relationships renders human life impossible. Bernard Berelson and Gary A. Steiner have said, "Total isolation is virtually always an intolerable situation for the human adult—even when physical needs are provided for."[6] Studies of infant mortality rates among children left in orphanages and handled, touched, or spoken to only infrequently indicate the importance of human relationships for our survival. Apart from such studies, Amitai Etzioni reinforces our understanding. "Human attributes grafted upon our biological base are difficult to sustain. Even without full isolation, they require continuous reinforcement or they will erode."[7] We are not self-grounded. The belief that we can be self-grounded and have the resources to find our true identity within us is a modern heresy.

Our selfhood does come to us as a gift. But it is not a gift that God buries deep within us and that we must then individually uncover. It comes to us through those means of grace that God's prevenience has always provided: our often flawed and sometimes destructive relationships with friends, family, and community.

A family in one congregation of which I have been a part once adopted two foster children who had been abused and neglected by their unwed, teenage moth-

19

er. She had locked them in an unfurnished room for most of the day while she looked for work or visited friends. Social service agencies finally intervened when the children, a boy and a girl, were two or three years old. The children were shuttled from one foster care situation to another for a period of time. The family I knew received the children at a point when no one else would take them. Both children had multiple physical and emotional problems. They suffered poor health because of their social deprivation, and they were nearly autistic. The children seemingly had developed a communication system of their own. They could communicate with each other, but they did not interact well with other children or adults. Exclusion and deprivation of human contact and social mutuality had left these children with diminished potential.

If our true identity is something self-grounded within us, something that we discover on our own exclusive of our relationships and commitments to other people, then these two children should have been very different than they were. In fact, it was the love and attention a particular couple lavished upon these two children that really brought them back to life. The resources they needed came to them through these two loving adults and their son. Selfhood was discovered not in lonely self-oriented quests inward but in mutuality and loving relationships with others.

"Beloved, let us love one another; for love is of God, and he who loves is born of God and knows God. He who does not love does not know God; for God is love. . . . No man has ever seen God; but if we love one another, God abides in us and love is perfected in us" (1 John 4:7-8, 12). God acted preveniently through that couple. God reached out and bestowed human worth upon those children through the loving relationships that developed over time. The children's worth was not something buried deep within that they had to struggle to uncover or recover. Their value and their identity were not a product manufactured out of the basic datum of their lives. It was a gift. Moreover, it was a free and gracious gift mediated through social life rather than individual self-orientation.

Franz Kafka's short story, "The Metamorphosis," expresses this same truth. The main character is a young man who leads an isolated and lonely life. He works in a job that does not provide him with opportunities to interact meaningfully with others. He commutes to and from work each day having little meaningful contact with others. Although he lives with his parents and family, he does not really connect emotionally with them, spending his evenings alone in his room.

One morning the man awakens to discover that he has become a giant cockroach. His horrified family gradually removes the human artifacts from his room: pictures, furniture, clothing. Eventually they stop giving him the same meals they eat, feeding him instead garbage and table scraps. By these actions, they insure that he will lose all contact with the human world of relationships. Such human contact might have restored him to humanity, Kafka suggests, but this human care is withheld. The young man does not have within his individual self the resources to restore his humanity; those who do have the resources—his family—are unwilling to share them with him. Consequently, he dies a pitiful, miserable death. Kafka is saying that our hold on human identity is quite tenuous and that we are not self-grounded creatures. Only our relationships and human commitments to one another enable us to remain fully human. Without them, we cease to be human beings at all.

Christian spirituality neglects this truth at its great

peril. When somehow we communicate that our true humanity is found only in the inner, private spaces of our hearts alone, we tread dangerously close to the heresy of self-groundedness. According to prevenient grace, our humanity is given to us through the tender ties of those who surround us in our social existence.

Doris Lessing, in her novel *The Summer before the Dark*, states this same truth. Kate, the main character, returns early from an overseas trip and cannot move back into her own home because the family has rented the house for the summer; she must seek temporary shelter elsewhere. She checks into a small, cheap hotel in a poor section of London. While there, she becomes seriously ill. Gradually she recovers, but she remains weak and haggard. Since she has always been an attractive woman who dressed stylishly, she is embarrassed to go out looking frail and worn, with her dresses hanging loosely upon her ravaged body. Much to her surprise, however, no one seems even to notice her. As a well-dressed, attractive woman she had always thrived on the attention of others around her. Now, she realizes, no one sees her at all when she is not attractive. This lack of attention from others leaves her feeling strangely sick. She feels as if she were a nonperson, invisible. A store clerk rings up her purchases, takes her money, and does not once look at her. She goes into a small Greek cafe. Again, "no one took any notice of her, though she had stiffened herself to take criticism. She knew now, she had to know at last, that all her life she had been held upright by an invisible fluid, the notice of other people."[8]

In our pure individuality we are invisible and unreal. The gift of personhood comes to us not through our striving to uncover the hidden gifts that God has buried deep within us; rather, it comes to us in the unexpected attention, care, and mutuality of our social relationships. True, such relationships can also cause distortions in our lives. True, such mutuality can warp our sense of self as we bend and accommodate ourselves to others or react in unhealthy ways to the demands of others. Yet such mutuality is essential to our humanity. We do not discover the gifts of God in our lives in isolation but in relationship and in mutuality with others.

The importance of our sociality and mutuality as God's means of grace is underlined by Walter Tubbs's "Beyond Perls." The dynamic process of spiritual formation is not a lonely exercise in self-grounding. It is a journey into deeper mutuality and joint discovery with others.

> *I do my thing and you do your thing.*
> *I am not in this world to live up to your expectations,*
> *And you are not in this world to live up to mine.*
> *You are you and I am I;*
> *If by chance we find each other, it's beautiful.*
> *If not, it can't be helped.*
>
> Fritz Perls

If I just do my thing and you do yours,
We stand in danger of losing each other
And ourselves.

I am not in this world to live up to your expectations;
But I am in this world to confirm you
As a unique human being.
And to be confirmed by you.

We are fully ourselves only in relation
   to each other;

Walter Tubbs, "Beyond Perls," *Journal of Humanistic Psychology*, Vol. 12, No. 2 (Fall 1972), p. 5. Copyright © 1972 by The Association for Humanistic Psychology, 416 Hoffman Avenue, San Francisco, CA 94114. Reprinted by permission of Sage Publications, Inc.

The I detached from a Thou
Disintegrates.

I do not find you by chance;
I find you by an active life
Of reaching out.

Rather than passively letting things happen
   to me,
I can act intentionally to make them happen.

I must begin with myself, true;
But I must not end with myself:
The truth begins with two.

We have been created by God for one another, in mutuality and partnership. We are truly our brother's and our sister's keepers. Participation in some ongoing patterns of social relatedness is essential to our spiritual journey. The companionship of others is an indispensible necessity for our existence before God and with God. Our humanity is a specification of communion among people. We are a "locus of communion." Thus, God is always calling us into communion, into companionship, into partnership with others. When we turn aside from such mutuality and regard others as incidental to our "interior" spiritual journey, we have gravely misunderstood God's prevenient means of grace.

Charles Wesley sings of this interpersonal dimension of prevenient grace in his hymn, "All Praise to Our Redeeming Lord":

All praise to our redeeming Lord,
Who joins us by his grace,
And bids us, each to each restored,
Together seek his face.

24

He bids us build each other up,
And, gathered into one,
To our high calling's glorious hope,
We hand in hand go on.

We all partake the joy of one;
The common peace we feel:
A peace to sensual minds unknown,
A joy unspeakable.

And if our fellowship below
In Jesus be so sweet,
What height of rapture shall we know
When round his throne we meet![9]

Our spiritual journeys require companions. While it is important to have those with whom we can share our most intimate, interior pilgrimages, it is equally— or perhaps even more—important that we have those with whom we share our everyday lives. We need more than just "spiritual friends." Such friends can sometimes seduce us into believing that the only important journey is the interior, private one that we may choose to share with a like-minded seeker. But we need to welcome all men and women into our lives. All those with whom we share sociality and mutuality are potential sources of God's prevenient grace. Our capacity to welcome such people into our lives and to receive spiritual gifts from those to whom our inner lives will always remain at a distance may determine our capacity for spiritual growth.

All of this struck me that day as I thumbed through those photographs of a world full of people to whom my life had become a stranger. I had tried to construct my identity and selfhood without reference to the sense of self with which these lives of family and friends had already gifted me. I did not need constantly to struggle to create or to discover some hidden true self. God was and is, throughout my whole life, gifting me with my selfhood in all moments of genuine welcoming and relationship.

Notes

1. Donald P. McNeill, Douglas A. Morrison, and Henri J. M. Nouwen, *Compassion* (Garden City, N.J.: Doubleday and Company, 1982), 20.

2. John E. Burkhart, *Worship* (Philadelphia: Westminster Press, 1982), 47-8.

3. James Fowler, *Becoming Adult, Becoming Christian* (San Francisco: Harper and Row, 1984), 99-101.

4. Abbé Huvelin, "Conference on Some of the Spiritual Guides of the Seventeenth Century," quoted in Baron Friedrich von Hügel, *Eternal Life* (Edinburgh: T & T Clark, 1913), 375-6.

5. "Talk of the Town," *The New Yorker* (13 February 1984), 18.

6. Barnard Berelson and Gary A. Steiner, *Human Behavior* (New York: Harcourt, Brace, and World, 1964), 252.

7. Amitai Etzioni, *An Immodest Agenda* (New York: McGraw Hill Book Company, 1983), 31.

8. Doris Lessing, *The Summer before the Dark* (New York: Alfred A. Knopf, 1973), 198.

9. Charles Wesley, "All Praise to Our Redeeming Lord," in *The Book of Hymns* (Nashville: The United Methodist Publishing House, 1966), no. 301.

TWO

We Are Our Brothers' and Sisters' Keepers

Somehow in our contemporary society we have come to believe that we must make a choice between our individual identity and our membership in groups or in social processes. We feel we need to sacrifice something of our own selfhood in order to belong in relationship and in mutuality with others. Our needs for self-fulfillment and for self-actualization must take a second place to the needs of the group. We believe that our individuality is something that we work out on our own; that it is totally unrelated to our social existence and our mutual partnerships with others.

It is possible, however, that individuality and participation in community are not mutually exclusive. In fact, it may be that our individual selfhood is actually guaranteed by our membership in groups and our relationships to others. Our human particularity is a product of our mutual welcomings among partners in a common humanity.

Most political rhetoric today depends upon a language of individual rights. Individuals have a right to fair housing, to accessibility, to equal education, to equal rights before the courts. This language of rights offers a rich storehouse for speaking of the claims that an individual may make on or against the collectivity, but it is relatively impoverished as a means of expressing the individual's needs *for* the collective experience with others.

We are, some would say, the first society in human history that assumes the individual rather than the family as the basic building block of social and political life. Our cultural heroes are all lonely individuals who stand against the social groups around them. We admire the tough, independent detective who operates by his or her own superior code of ethics and is constantly harrassed by those who place group loyalty above individual conscience. Somehow, we think that one can be a truly good person only if one resists fully joining the group. Our traditions of Christian ethics speak of "moral man and immoral society," as if individuals can act in moral ways while groups are always tainted. Our moral integrity can be saved only when we resist becoming part of the group. It is one thing to leave our parents and cleave to our spouses, as Genesis 2:24 advises. It is entirely a different matter when our individualistic culture obscures the fact that our lives begin in and owe much to our original families, even as we grow toward individuation.

Families bring up their own children in ways that encourage the children to "leave home," to deny their own psychological and emotional rootedness. The biologically normal dependency of children upon adults is somehow seen as abnormal. This, in turn, encourages children to have considerable amnesia about what they owe to their parents. We are, in effect, encouraged to see ourselves as giving birth to ourselves, as being our own parents.

Our national myth encourages this same denial of our need for community. This is the "New World." Those who came here left behind their roots. Those who arrived on these shores made a new start. We do not owe anything to the past. This national self-understanding has encouraged us to see ourselves as a people who owe nothing to those tender social relationships that have bestowed identity upon us and that, through memories and hopes, help tell us who we are. The most dangerous aspect of this is that we have become a people who not only deny owing anything to our collective past but, by the same logic, accept no responsibility to our future. Thus, we are willing to mortgage our future in tremendous national debts and unfaced ecological and social problems or to threaten future generations with nuclear annihilation.

Such is the grip that the heresy of self-groundedness has upon us. Adam and Eve seek to eat the forbidden fruit in order that they may know even the knowledge of good and evil. They want to be completely self-sufficient. The fruit, they hope, will give them all the resources they will ever need to live their lives on their own.

Christianity's trinitarian language itself reflects an alternative understanding: relationship and community are prior to individuality. The sharing and the reciprocity between the three persons of the trinity give a separate uniqueness and identity to each one. The technical use of personae for the three aspects of the trinity also suggests this relationship between social exchanges and individual selfhood. *Persona* is a theater term for character. It implies involvement in social drama, in the giving and receiving of communal existence. Just as the Father, Son, and Holy Spirit have a

29

personality because they are social partners who welcome one another, so the individual Christian has a personal identity, a self, because he or she is involved in networks of sociality. George C. Lodge has summed up this situation well: "By connoting his participation in the interaction and drama of life, the idea of the personality emphasized the social nature of man and his place in a community as basic to a man's separate life. The whole man and his fulfillment depended not merely upon the individual self but upon the many relationships between the individual and those around him."[1]

Christianity's most central dogma affirms that somehow our individuality flows from our participation in social networks and human relationships. Our identity begins in our mutuality and in our common existence. We are not self-made, self-grounded creatures. In fact, when we are reduced merely to individuals, we are prey to the most demonic and destructive dimensions of life. Our claims to basic "rights" depends not upon our individuality but upon our basic sociality.

Our century has experimented with what it means to be a bare individual, stripped of a rootedness in sociality. Think of the prison and concentration camps that dotted northern and eastern Europe and that still dot Siberia, South Africa, or sections of Asia. To these places came those who had been fathers, sons, neighbors, and friends. Each one came with a history and with an identity rooted in his or her relatedness to others. These relationships were what made them real people worthy of respect and of honor. But within these barbed-wire rectangles, they were stripped of clothing, glasses, wedding rings, and all those other reminders of the relationships that had made them separate, individual human beings. They were broken

down into units of pure individuality. We see the
results. Where there is no family, no tribe, no congregation, no neighborhod, there is nothing but the demonic. Here is an example of what happened in
Germany under the Nazis: "When a Jew could no
longer appeal to his fellow German as a neighbour, as a
friend, as a relation, as a partner, as a fellow Jew even,
when at the end, naked at the barbed wire, he could
only appeal to the man with the whip as a fellow
human being, then it was more than too late. When
men confront each other as men, as abstract univer-
sals, one with power, the other with none, then man is
certain to behave as a wolf to his own kind."[2]

The problem is not to defend the individual against
the collective, but to so ground the individual in the
communal that each person becomes real, historic,
and significant, with the social relationships and partnerships to protect himself or herself. Thus, early Israel always began with the nation, not with the individual. Thus, the early church always began with the
body of Christ, with the New Israel, with the community of faith.

The early church's struggle with the Gnostics was
largely an attempt to assert that community is the only
guarantee of individual identity that can be trusted. To
early Christian apologists such as Ireneaus of Lyons,
the Gnostics were a threat because they asserted that
individual identity could be maintained apart from all
human mutuality. Christian life, Ireneaus stated, is a
life predicated upon a sharing of life among a people of
God. Summing up Ireneaus's teaching, Rowan Williams wrote, "The goal of Christian growth is a knowledge of God entirely founded in a sharing of life, an
intimacy between persons, the fellowship of God with
human beings in their humanness."[3]

Saint Augustine emphasized again and again how

31

our individuality is guaranteed by our partnerships with others in community. His classic spiritual autobiography, *The Confessions*, is a testimony to the molding and shaping of personality through various social and relational exchanges and through the different dimensions of mutuality and partnership. Augustine's legacy is an awareness of the conditional character of human behavior. The groups, relationships, and social networks in which we live, move, and have our being are powerful shapers of our identity and selfhood.

Augustine played a major role in shaping and reshaping the monastic traditions as vehicles of human and Christian transformation. His most explicit thoughts about the relationships between individuality and community are contained in a letter that he wrote to some nuns who were organizing a religious community. Augustine argued that the requirement of the community life of faith, charity, and mutual service among the community's members was the method most likely to bring about wholeness.[4] Individual wholeness lay in the perfecting of the total community's life. Holiness in the community was intimately related to human wholeness as expressed in mutual welcomings among men and women. The common life was the primary means through which individual lives could be sanctified. Augustine's thought played a major role in transforming monasticism from an independent or semi-independent life pursued by solitary Christians into a shared partnership in communal discovery.

John Cassian, the other major formulator of western monasticism, built upon Augustine's work. Even after Augustine, most monks continued to see the communal life as a training school in the spiritual life. The monk intended to graduate from community and become a "mature" Christian who lived as a solitary hermit. Cassian, who may have come to appreciate the value of community after his sojourn in the Egyptian desert, argued against such a belief. Rather, Cassian claimed, community life was a lifetime goal in its own right.[5]

Benedict of Nursia codified the scattered works of Cassian, Augustine, and others. His *Rule* has shaped much of western monasticism. Through the monastic experiment, Benedict's ideals have penetrated most traditional forms of western spirituality. The whole Anglican tradition, from which the Wesleys derived their spiritual lives, is considered by some commentators to be a remarkable attempt to make the ideals of Benedictine monasticism apply to all Christians, lay and ordained.[6]

Benedict's *Rule* opens with an attack upon those monks who seek God apart from community and mutuality. These are monks who live alone and travel from place to place, seeking their own individual fulfillment. They are "restless, servants to the seduction of their own will and appetites," Benedict states. Also, there are Sarabaites, who live alone or in small traveling groups. "Their only law is the pleasure of their desires."[7] These descriptions still apply today. The end result of a lonely pursuit for selfhood apart from community is a deep restlessness. Without the roots of community and relationship to help us know a stable sense of self, we are always restless. Encouraged to dismantle and to discard the aspects of our personal histories that are the history of relatedness to others in communal partnerships, we are easily seduced and confused.

Benedict sets over against these monks the Cenobites who live together in community. The Cenobites, he concludes, "are the best kind of monks."[8] Benedict's most important vow is that of stability, in which the monk agrees to live perpetually with a group of other men or women in an ongoing community of memory and of hope. It is through daily life in community that individual holiness and sanctification are achieved. Moreover, the bonds of community guarantee each monk's individuality and protect each monk from exploitation and from seduction.

> It is [Benedict's] new understanding of the relationship between the members of the community that is the great breakthrough. The older ideal had been essentially that of the novice finding a holy man and asking to learn from him, and the monastery had been a group of individuals gathered round the feet of a sage. One of these earlier rules, the Rule of the Master, had given enormous power to the abbot. St. Benedict changes this almost exclusively vertical pattern of authority by emphasizing the relationships of the monks with each other.[9]

Individuality and community or collectivity are not opposites to be set against each other. They are two poles of one reality that each requires the other. We are not dealing with two opposing conceptions, but with a fundamental tension in human existence between the experience of separation and the experience of connection. "There are truths we do not see when we adopt the language of radical individualism. We find ourselves not independently of other people and institutions but through them. We never get to the bottom of our selves on our own. We discover who we are face to face and side by side with others in work, love, and learning. All of our activity goes on in relationships, groups, associations, and communities."[10] Our sense of individual worth, personal dignity, and ethical autonomy is in fact dependent upon a thousand unseen social, relational, and communal ties. We discover ourselves as men and as women before God through the welcoming of one another into our lives. "The more persistently and effectively a man responds to his response to his neighbor, the more clearly there are both communion and individuality, both of which are indispensible for human existence."[11] We will never achieve our goals of Christian growth so long as we attempt to meet them apart from community. We need more than the resources of our own interior lives. We need more than the resources of a few like-minded spiritual friends. We need the support of a community of people who are both like us and different from us. We need the resources of strangers and friends alike, both of whom we must learn to welcome into our own spiritual journeys as companions.

Browne Barr recently has compared the life of the Christian community to a flock of geese. Barr's interest in this comparison stems from a brief sermon illustration about geese and the church that he overheard in a sermon one Sunday. He decided to check the illustration out with an ornithologist. He discovered the analogy was accurate. The formation of geese in flight improves aerodynamic efficiency. Theoretically, twenty-five birds have a range increase of approximately 70 percent as compared to a goose flying alone. A flock of geese flying together can travel 70 percent farther than a goose flying alone. Geese fly faster and farther in formation than they do one by one.[12]

The solitary Christian is often self-affirming and self-congratulating. Like the solitary, heroic cowboy or detective, the solitary Christian is apt to feel that he or she is leading a purer, more noble Christian life than all those who follow the herd instinct and congregate in churches. "The church is full of hypocrites. I can get closer to God on my own." "Those people aren't really interested in getting to know Jesus, so I can't be bothered with them." "If just some more people in that church had an experience of the Holy Spirit like I did, maybe they would wake up." Such Christians are absolutely certain that they are traveling farther and faster than the plodding groups of sinners that gather together in worship and in study. Yet are they really journeying upon their solitary pilgrimage that much faster?

John Bunyan offers two contrasting images of the pilgrim's journey to God. The first is found in the beginning part of *Pilgrim's Progress*. Christian's journey is essentially a solitary one. He must leave home in order to begin his journey, so he sets off and separates himself from the familiar relationships of family and neighborhood. While other travelers or companions appear beside him from time to time, they are not true fellow journeyers. They are more like a collection of individuals all on the same road at the same time.

The second part of Bunyan's work, however, was written when Bunyan was an older and more mature Christian. Here the heroine, Christiana, travels with true companions. The risks of the journey are shared by all the pilgrims together. The moments of doubt and uncertainty are alleviated by joint consultation and collegiality. Their shared journey is itself a foretaste of the shared, communal life of the Celestial City.

We often read the first half of Bunyan's work and ignore the second part. We are enamored of the individual journey and seldom recognize our need for partnership with others who are different from us. If the kingdom of God is always pictured as a social kingdom, full of mutuality and sociality, why do we think that we must journey there alone? Surely our pilgrimage to the heavenly city must prepare us for life there. If we travel alone and never learn the skills of partnership with others in Christ, then adjustment to life in the kingdom will certainly be difficult at best. Should not our pilgrimage be both foretaste and preparation for our destination?

Even the oft-repeated Protestant emphasis upon the priesthood of all believers has served to accentuate this individualistic bias. We have understood this concept to mean that we are all our own priests before God. Yet this is hardly what Luther meant. For Luther, the priesthood of all believers meant that we were to be priests for one another. The priesthood of all believers does not mean that we are competent to deal with God for ourselves. It means rather that we are called and responsible to deal with God on behalf of our neighbor. We are priests to each other, not priests to ourselves.

For Luther, we are called to be agents of judgment and of mercy for one another. There can be no priest who stands in the midst of a congregation if members of that congregation are not already priests to each other. There can be no sacramental means of grace within the congregation if the members are not means of grace to one another.

Our mutual priesthoods operate in several ways. First, we are means of grace to one another in that our life in community protects our moments of solitude. It also protects us from being infringed upon by misguided togetherness. Through community we are the guardians of each other's solitude.

> Community is always poised between two poles: solitude and togetherness. Without togetherness community disperses; without solitude community collapses into a mass, a crowd. But solitude and togetherness are not mutually antagonistic; on the contrary, they make each other possible. Solitude without togetherness deteriorates into loneliness. One needs

37

strong roots in togetherness to be solitary rather than
lonely when one is alone. . . . Togetherness without
solitude is not truly togetherness, but rather side-by-
sideness. To live merely side by side is alienation. We
need time and space to be alone, to find ourselves in
solitude, before we can give ourselves to one another in
true togetherness.[13]

Community protects us from the alienation of being
one member of a herd, of being just another number in
mass society. In this sense, community protects us
from the demonic powers that would destroy all individuality and identity. Community keeps us located in
lasting relationships and meaningful commitments in
such a way that we have some open spaces in our lives
for solitude. It protects us from the restlessness that
Saint Benedict saw in the wandering hermits.

We are means of grace to one another in a second
way. When we learn to welcome those people who are
strangers into our lives, we also strengthen our ability
to welcome unseen, hidden aspects of our inner
selves. Pursuing a solitary Christian pilgrimage that
prevents us from recognizing other men and women
as our partners in a common humanity allows us to
ignore our need to make peace with those aspects of
our personality that we dislike or find unacceptable.
We can avoid acknowledging those parts of our personality that do not fit with our own self-image so long
as we can isolate ourselves from other people who
possess such unacceptable, unacknowledged behaviors. We can hide from our inner contradictions behind the walls of private life, behind the masks that we
wear. But in public, social life, we are drawn out into
the open. We need to interact with others in our spiritual journeys. Without these strangers who journey
with us, we might never become aware of those inner
blocks and tensions that must be faced if we are to

grow. Without such strangers in our lives, we can carefully avoid facing the distortions that must be faced if we are to discover who we really are before God.

Certainly, coercive and manipulative groups have always distorted the lives of Christian people by their practices. Sometimes the pressure to conform has been so intense that people have denied that within them which was real and genuinely of Christ in order to win approval or to avoid punishment and ostracism.

Yet in our time and in our society, the risks of individualism are far greater. Our lives as those who are made in God's image are far more likely to be distorted by the excesses of individualism than by the problems of communal, relational existence. More people are likely to become lost and entrapped in the false self spun from too much isolation and self-preoccupation than are likely to become distorted by community life. "Christians are most in the Spirit when they stand at the crossing point of the inward and the outward life. And at that intersection, community is found. Community is a place where the connections felt in our hearts make themselves known in the bonds between people."[14]

Individuality and community are inexorably linked. We cannot approach God without also approaching our very human brothers and sisters. And this does not mean just a few, carefully selected brothers and sisters who are close spiritual friends and therefore mirror images of us. It means the mixed multitude of friends, acquaintances, and strangers that we encounter daily in our groups, associations, and institutions. Our specifically Christian communities ought to contain enough diversity and strangeness to instruct and train us in receiving all people as potential partners in a common humanity.

Community is a constant theme in the hymns of

Charles and John Wesley. The interpersonal and the intrapersonal experiences are intertwined. The growing presence of a catholic spirit of openness and hospitality to all people is an important sign of authentic spiritual experience. In one hymn, Charles Wesley speaks of the lodestone—the magnet—of God's love that draws us individually closer to God but also draws us closer to one another.

> Jesus, united by thy grace,
> And each to each endeared,
> With confidence we seek thy face,
> And know our prayer is heard.
>
> Help us to help each other, Lord,
> Each other's cross to bear.
> Let each his friendly aid afford,
> And feel his brother's care.
>
> Up unto thee, our living Head,
> Let us in all things grow,
> Till thou hast made us free indeed
> And spotless here below.
>
> Touched by the lodestone of thy love,
> Let all our hearts agree;
> And ever toward each other move,
> And ever move toward thee.[15]

In another hymn, Wesley links this experience of God's grace with a catholic spirit, a hospitality that is open to God's prevenience in all people and events:

> Forth in thy name, O Lord, I go,
> My daily labor to pursue;
> Thee, only thee, resolved to know
> In all I think or speak or do.

The task thy wisdom hath assigned,
O let me cheerfully fulfill;
In all my works thy presence find,
And prove thy good and perfect will.[16]

These hymns have several implications for the contemporary American church. First, they imply that our neglect and rejection of the traditional, basic trinitarian images may be related to our inability to understand how relationships in community are linked to individuality. This is a vicious circle. The less we use trinitarian images, the less appreciation we have for community as the matrix of our true individuality. Similarly, the less community seems to give birth to a deep sense of personal centeredness, the less meaningfully we can use the trinitarian formulas. Our unbridled individualism leads us to abandon the dynamic faith in a living, active, trinitarian God. Thus we often end up with a God who lacks the power and presence to change our lives.

Second, we need to rethink how God's means of grace intersect human experience. This requires more careful attention to our language, metaphors, and analogies. Often I have been left with the feeling that God somehow loved me in isolation from my relatedness to others. I am left with the feeling that God speaks to me directly, never through other men and women. When someone tells me that I am a "King's kid" or a royal child of God, they leave me with the feeling that I am somehow so from birth. Yet often the means of grace through which I have genuinely been made to feel special to God have come through other people. The key images and words of Christian faith—words such as *salvation, forgiveness,* or *grace*—remain flat and somehow artificial until they are fleshed out by living encounters with other people.

41

I suspect I had never really understood what for-giveness was until one weekend I was asked to watch someone's dog. I had understood the concept of for-giveness. I had used the word. But it took a relational encounter with another person before I felt forgive-ness incarnated in my life.

I had been asked to watch someone's dog over a Saturday night. I had been asked because the owner knew that I was very fond of dogs and that I had a small cairn terrier myself. All I had to do was remember to take the dog for a walk in the morning and then in the evening and to check the bowl to make sure that there was water and food. It was important, however, to remember to walk the dog. Like most humans, a dog can wait only so long after eating before the pressures of nature build up within its body. I said I would walk the dog. But I forgot. I was busy. I had many things to do. I was tired. It simply slipped my mind. It was not part of my usual routine. I could have made a thou-sand excuses. The simple fact is that I woke up the next morning and realized that I had forgotten to do a job I promised to do. I knew what the consequences would be. I wondered what had greeted my friends as they opened the door and walked in. No, I didn't wonder what they had found. I wondered what they would think of me.

I was sure that they would not speak to me, that they would be completely unable to understand why I had not done what I said I would do. In fact, *I* could not even understand why I had not done what I said I would do. But I worked up my courage and drove to their house later that day. I paused in the car and wondered if I should just drive off; better they should never speak to me again. But I got out, went to the door, rang the bell and waited. The door opened. There was a moment of awkward silence. Before I had an opportunity to say, "I'm sorry," I was given a big hug and told, "You're still my friend."

In that moment I understood something about forgiveness and acceptance that all my self-preoccupation and individual inner explorations had never taught me. In fact, my inner, interior experiences had taught me more about judgment and lack of acceptance than about forgiveness and grace. I could never have understood something very basic to Christian faith in my isolation. It took an experience in community, with partners and with strangers, to learn about forgiveness.

We need to recover a language of community in our Christian congregations. We need to help people discover the ways that their individual lives and Christian journeys are illuminated not by preoccupation with their own lives but by encounters with other people.

> Most of us fear community because we think it will call us away from ourselves. We are afraid that in community our sense of self will be overpowered by the identity of the group. . . . We have forgotten that the self is a moving intersection of many other selves. We are formed by the lives which intersect ours. The larger and richer our community, the larger and richer is the content of the self. There is no individuality without community. . . . So the way to self, and to self-health, is the way of community. We have lost a true sense of self in our time because we have lost community.[17]

We need to help people understand that the priesthood of believers does not mean that they are priests to themselves but rather that they are priests to one another.

The third implication is that a renewed emphasis upon the importance of sociality and mutuality for our individual selfhood may draw us out of our spiritual

43

narcissism. A kind of self-righteousness often creeps into our emphasis upon our individual pilgrimages. It is as if we feel we are responsible for our journeys ourselves. Only with difficulty do we acknowledge the role that other people—both friends and strangers—play in mediating God's grace and growth to us or in helping us grasp more fully the deepest affirmations of the Christian faith.

> The gentlest form of spiritual narcissism is the idea that one can accomplish one's own spiritual growth. . . . The belief that "I can do it" is intimately associated with the assumption that "it is my idea, my desire, to do it." Although we have made a strong case here for a primary human desire for union and unconditional love, we have also maintained that this desire is not of a solely human origin or source. . . . The striving, even if we try to own it, was planted in us. It comes from somewhere very deep, from a depth at which one can no longer say, "This is me and only me."[18]

We will grow in grace not when we isolate ourselves from others and pay only a passing compliment to the community of Christian faith. We will grow in grace when we place ourselves regularly and faithfully in that mixed multitude of saints and sinners, of strangers and spiritual friends that we find in the average Christian congregation.

Notes

1. George C. Lodge, *The New American Ideology* (New York: Alfred A. Knopf, 1975), 55.

2. Michael Ignatieff, *The Needs of Strangers* (New York: Viking, 1985), 52.

3. Rowan Williams, *Christian Spirituality* (Atlanta: John Knox, 1979), 28.

4. *The Rule of St. Benedict*, trans. Anthony C. Meisel and M.L. del Mastro (Garden City, N.J.: Doubleday and Company, Image Books, 1975), 20.

5. *St. Benedict*, 24.

6. Esther de Waal, *Seeking God* (Collegeville, MN.: Liturgical Press, 1984), 22–3.

7. *St. Benedict*, 47.

8. *St. Benedict*, 47.

9. de Waal, 18–19.

10. Robert N. Bellah et al., *Habits of the Heart* (Berkeley: University of California Press, 1985), 84.

11. Joseph Haroutunian, *God with Us* (Philadelphia: Westminster Press, 1965), 151.

12. Browne Barr, *High Flying Geese* (Minneapolis: Seabury Press, 1983), 19.

13. David Steindl-Rast, *A Listening Heart* (New York: Crossroad, 1983), 24.

14. Parker J. Palmer, *The Promise of Paradox* (Notre Dame: Ave Maria Press, 1980), 88.

15. Charles Wesley, "Jesus, United by Thy Grace," in *The Book of Hymns*, no. 193.

16. Charles Wesley, "Forth in Thy Name," in *The Book of Hymns*, no. 152.

17. Palmer, 73–4.

18. Gerald G. May, *Will and Spirit* (San Francisco: Harper and Row, 1982), 115.

THREE

*Jesus Came to Eat and Drink
with Sinners*

Over the years I have been in many, many homes of religious people. Often these families will have a picture of Jesus hanging somewhere in their rooms. For some families or individuals this picture will portray the Sacred Heart of Jesus, in which Jesus is shown with a large heart visible upon his chest, the heart enveloped in flames. Other households seem to prefer Sallman's "Head of Christ," with its soft brown tones and gentle light falling on Jesus' shoulder-length hair. More and more younger families often have an etching in black and white of Jesus with his head thrown back and a broad, laughing smile spread across his face.

As I browse through religious book stores, I notice the numbers of these pictures of Jesus that hang on the wall. Invariably, however, Jesus is alone. One sketch has a powerful Jesus planing a block of wood in his carpenter's shop. Another has Jesus holding a few tiny lambs against a background of blue skies and green pastures. But he is always alone. For whom is he planing that block of wood? Will it be a table at which he will be invited to share a meal? Who has made him break into the broad smile? We seldom laugh all by ourselves. Did someone tell a joke? Play a prank?

I can think of only one exception to this tendency to portray Jesus all alone. On my grandparents' dining room wall, hung directly above my grandfather's rolltop desk, was a copy of da Vinci's "The Last Supper." Here Jesus is surrounded by his friends and companions. Here, at least, we see him doing what the Gospels frequently suggest he always did: eat and drink and share his life with others around him.

Why do we always picture Jesus alone? These pictures of a solitary Jesus have a profound impact upon our spiritual lives. They suggest that we can have Jesus all for ourselves. We alone are in the shop with him as he works at the bench. It is with us alone that he laughs, delighted with our company. The messages of these pictures, paintings, and sketches encourage us to see Jesus all alone except for us.

Yet that focus is all wrong. It is not faithful to the verbal pictures of Jesus that we find in the Gospels. Certainly, Jesus did go apart. "He went away to a lonely place and prayed," we are frequently told. Most of the Gospels, however, describe Jesus as one who restored men and women to life by restoring them to communion with others. Jesus is the one who saves men and women by welcoming them into communion, into mutuality and partnership.

If we become fully human and if we come to possess a sense of selfhood and identity through our relatedness to others, then to be deprived of communion with others is to be condemned to a living death. If we never discover who we are except side-by-side in living relationships, then those who are excluded from such partnerships and social recognition are reduced to invisible nonpersons. Death reigns where men and women are excluded from the relationships and associations that help them discover who they are as God's children. Salvation from death and from finitude comes when strangers welcome one another and acknowledge their common humanity.

"Human nature" is the specification of communion among people. We have come to have it and know it as such in that communion among creatures that is called "love." It is the manner of human existence and action. Human beings, at once as subjects and objects, acting and acted upon, emerge and become aware of others and of themselves in a continued communion that is the condition of each man's existence as well as of his "nature." The loving and not-loving of my fellowman is to me literally a matter of life and death as a human being. I continue to exist as this man because I am loved as this man—not as one who has been loved, or is loved occasionally, but as one who draws his life constantly from the recognition of his neighbor and the communion that goes with it.

If salvation issues from communion with God through our communion with other men and women, then sin becomes the turning away from communion, from the human means of grace through which we might be restored to God's intentions for us. Sin becomes the erecting of boundaries that separate us from one another. To sin is to refuse to welcome the other person into our lives. ". . . sin is the death of man because sin is the breaking up of communion by which men exist and live and have peace."[1]

Sin is alienation. It is the refusal to acknowledge the claims another person makes upon us for recognition. If we can discover who we are truly created to be only when we are involved in the give-and-take of human relationships with both friends and strangers, then to deprive someone of such acceptance and recognition is sin and death.

> O Lord, who shall sojourn in your tent?
> Who shall dwell on thy holy hill?
> He who walks blamelessly, and does what is right,
>   and speaks truth from his heart;
> who does not slander with his tongue,
>   and does no evil to his friend,
>   nor takes up a reproach against his neighbor.
> —Psalm 15:1-3

> Thus says the Lord:
> "For the three transgressions of Israel,
>   and for four, I will not revoke the punishment,
> because they sell the righteous for silver,
>   and the needy for a pair of shoes—
> they that trample the head of the poor into the dust of the
>   earth,
>   and turn aside the way of the afflicted;
> a man and his father go in to the same maiden,
>   so that my holy name is profaned;
> they lay themselves down beside every altar
>   upon garments taken in pledge;
> and in the house of their God they drink
>   the wine of those who have been fined."
> —Amos 2:6-8

Salvation, on the other hand, breaks into human experience when we come together with others in mutual recognition and establish life-giving relationships that help us define who we are. The Passover meal celebrates God's saving and redeeming of Israel. In it, both stranger and sojourner are recognized as equals with the Israelite. Salvation occurs and sinful death is defeated when strangers welcome one another within community. "If a stranger sojourns among you, and will keep the passover to the Lord, . . . according to its ordinance, so shall he do; you shall have one statute, both for the sojourner and for the native" (Num. 9:14).

This openness to the stranger and sojourner was not just limited to the passover. It also applied to other ritual and liturgical gatherings. If a sojourning stranger wished to offer sacrifices to Israel's God, the stranger was allowed to do so. The stranger was also not excluded from the congregation. "As you are, so shall the sojourner be before the Lord. One law and one ordinance shall be for you and for the stranger who sojourns with you" (Num. 15:15-6). Nor is the sojourning outsider to suffer from discrimination. No wrong shall be done to a stranger simply because of the status as a stranger. "When a stranger sojourns with you in your land, you shall not do him wrong. The stranger who sojourns with you shall be to you as the native among you, and you shall love him as yourself" (Lev. 19:33). We form partnerships, at the most basic level, in order to confer humanity upon one another and to sustain one another in that genuine human existence.

Throughout his ministry, Jesus' actions continually sought to reach out to men and women, including them in relationships with one another and with him. He never seemed to invite others into relationship with himself without also inviting them into relationship with one another. For Jesus the reign of God was social and relational. His acts of inclusion and recognition were signs of this coming reign.

Jesus' table fellowship, recalled in the da Vinci painting that hung above my grandfather's desk, became the moment in which Jesus' intentional recognition of men and women took place. Jesus extended himself to "those who lived on the margins of society because of their material and/or spiritual poverty, their ritually

51

unclean professions, or their public sins. . . . Jesus'
community offered a welcoming place where they
could feel honored as children of God apart from the
niches they had fallen into at birth or carved out for
themselves over the years."[2] That Jesus ate and drank
with sinners becomes the characteristic feature of his
ministry. Such activity overcomes barriers that isolate
and separate individuals from one another. It restores
the possibility of human acceptance and establishes
the opportunity to discover our identity as children of
God.

To eat and drink with sinners was to establish new
bonds of life betweeen those who had been living in
the kingdom of death and Jesus. As Elizabeth Schüssler Fiorenza points out, it is insufficient to understand
tax collectors, sinners, and prostitutes as mere moral
categories. These individuals lived beyond society's
boundaries. They were excluded and marginalized
people before they were "sinners." Exclusion from
acceptance and from relationships in community
meant that they lacked identity as "real" people. This
lack of status and identity is what drove them into
occupations and activities that were dishonorable. As
invisible nonpersons they had no legitimate method to
make their way in the world.[3]

Although Luke 19 suggests that all tax collectors
were rich, Fiorenza argues that in fact most of those
who did the actual work of collecting taxes were quite
poor. They were de facto slaves of oppressive tax agencies. Most prostitutes in the ancient world likewise
were impoverished and unskilled. Often they were
slaves, young women sold or rented out by other
family members. They were the divorced and the wid-
owed, the abandoned and the captive. They were women who had no established position in society,
lacking identities that made them visible, truly human

selves. Without such relational recognition and communal identity, these women could be easily exploited and relegated to subhuman positions or roles. They were reduced to units of pure individuality.[4] Most so-called sinners were those who lacked access to the social memberships and roles that could legitimate their human existence. They were, therefore, open to exploitation and abuse. In first-century Judaism, sinners were those who could not keep the Torah and hence were excluded from communal memberships that would have authenticated their lives. Modern readers hardly grasp this sociological dimension to the term *sinner*. Our moralizing and pious understandings have blocked a deeper appreciation for what marginalized, invisible nonpersons must do just to survive. These "sinners" were driven into poorly paid, exploitive positions: fruit-sellers, swine-herders, servants, and other service occupations; all deemed polluting and unclean.[5]

These men and women could not participate regularly in relationships and communal settings where recognition as partners in a common humanity could be established. They were invisible to themselves because they were invisible to others. Without others to recognize them as people of value, worth, and God-given identity, they could not experience themselves as people of worth, value, or identity. In fact, Jewish law excluded them from the one place where such recognition was most visible and important: table-fellowship. Strict interpretations of Torah, promulgated by social and religious elites, excluded marginalized people from table-fellowship. The Torah's dietary regulations became both the expression of and the means to exclusion and denial of human recognition. A number of practices and institutions fostered this double burden upon "sinners." Such practices denied marginal people any social acceptance. At the same time, denial of this social acceptance deprived them of the religious resources to feel acceptable to God and to themselves.

Haberim, or associations of pious Jews, regularly met in homes to practice Torah regulations of tithes and purity at meals. Originally, these regulations had applied only to the temple precincts. As Judaism became more and more concerned with being a "holy people," however, the regulations were gradually applied to all situations and people. Exclusion from such pious associations denied membership recognition to people who could not observe such strict practices because of their lifestyle or occupation.

While this tendency toward exclusion operated among many groups of scribes and Pharisees, it reached its apex in the Qumran covenanteers. These separatists withdrew entirely from the Jewish mainstream and retired to the wilderness. They sought to live apart from the "children of darkness." Membership was zealously protected by elaborate membership procedures that made a clear distinction between insiders and outsiders, between acceptable people who were valued by God and invisible nonpersons. Even among the Qumran covenanteers table-fellowship was a key sign of who was a real person loved by God and who was an unacceptable nonperson.[6]

Table-fellowship is a powerful expression of, as well as a means to, communal recognition because eating and drinking together are basic to human existence. Sharing a meal is a basic affirmation of humanity over animality. Behind the rules and regulations of first-century Judaism lies a very basic truth about what makes us human. Our capacity to share with others, our ability to draw near through relationships to others is what distinguishes us from animals.

> Shared meals, when taken together by choice, do express human relationships. Animals grab a hunk of meat and scamper off to gnaw on it by themselves, or animals crowd each other in the trough; while in virtually every culture, humans congregate companionately to eat. Eating and drinking are not simply biological activities. They express the very texture of human association. Sharing a meal is a vital symbol of social solidarity. Meals express relationships, and they also constitute them.[7]

Table-fellowship is a powerful expression of the relational character of human existence. It can establish the bonds among people that constitute a human community. Therefore, people of all ages and cultures have guarded table-fellowship by complex and rigid regulations.

Our meals together express our memberships and our partnerships. They affirm the boundaries that include some people in a common humanity and that exclude others. Thus, meals in a restaurant once confirmed the racial segregation of American society.

Even our own lives are governed by complex rules of table-fellowship. For acquaintances and co-workers whom we do not know well, we have a party. There will be cold drinks that each person pours for himself or herself. At most there will be finger foods or small sandwiches that each person picks up and eats on a plate. We do not sit down for a meal together. We stand around the room or the house. There are people whom we would invite to a party such as this but whom we would never invite to sit down for an evening dinner.

We must know people very well in order to eat with them at a table. There is a risk in eating together. What if a bite of food falls off the fork? What if something slips out of my mouth? Or a glass spills? There is a risk of looking slightly ridiculous and embarrassed. We will not take that risk with just anyone. Moreover, there is some sense of exposure when we eat. We open our mouths to one another and expose ourselves in ways that are not always attractive. There is a different relationship involved when we have table-fellowship with someone. Couples will often eat together when they are dating and trying to establish a relationship with each other.

When we think about eating together in this way, Jesus' table-fellowship with those who were excluded nonpersons suddenly takes on new meaning. Jesus' offer of table-fellowship was a sign of salvation and acceptance to those who were not acceptable. Think back to the last time you did not receive the invitation to dinner that everyone else in your office received. Remember the last time you were not invited to that second cousin's wedding. That feeling of not counting, of not making a difference, of being excluded was what Torah regulations of table-fellowship did to many first-century men and women. They were left as unreal, invisible nonpersons who had no sense of selfhood because they were excluded from the social relationships and mutual recognition that could help them feel someone had "seen" them as real people.

The importance of table-fellowship for establishing and confirming our partnerships in a common humanity was illustrated in a *Boston Globe* column. The author, Linda Weltner, was frequently apart from her husband. His father was dying in Florida, and he had to make regular trips there to assist his mother with medical questions and to settle up accounts and business affairs after his father's death. Linda Weltner arrived at the airport after each of these journeys in order to meet her husband as he exited from the expected late-evening flight. Their welcoming each other became more a welcoming between strangers than a reunion of husband and wife. "We greet each other across the distance of time spent apart and experiences unshared, two guarded individuals taking one another's measure. We need something to help us heal the pain of separation, to enable us to reconnect emotionally," she writes.

That "something" turns out to be food. It is a shared meal. "To tell you the truth, we need to eat." Sharing a meal enables Weltner and her husband to bridge the separation and isolation between them. Sharing a meal makes their relationship more visible. "And as we eat, we talk. And as we eat and talk, we grow more comfortable with one another. Soon I recognize the man across from me as the husband who left me on Monday and returned. And I take on a familiar configuration as Florida recedes in his eyes," she confesses.

Finally, she concludes, "This is more a celebration than a meal. When we savor what is set before us, not only our palates, but our hearts, our minds, our selves leave the table satisfied. There is a history within us which resonates when we eat, a physical as well as a mental collection of familial memories and feelings that are stirred up with each bite. It is little wonder that !!!FOOD!!! has the power to comfort the lonely, the abandoned, the grieving child in all of us."[8]

Welcoming others at table with us is how we bestow mutual recognition upon one another. It affirms existing social relationships that confer an identity and a selfhood upon us. It can also establish these relationships.

First-century Judaism clearly understood this dimension of table-fellowship. It invested meals with rituals and regulations that intensified this natural capacity of eating together to make people feel as if they are persons or nonpersons. Thus, Jesus' most radical act was to show hospitality at table. He is remembered most for eating and drinking with sinners. Excluded men and women who had been labeled "sinners" precisely because they were excluded, marginalized nonpersons were invited into relationships with one another through table-fellowship with Jesus.

Jesus shared a meal with Zacchaeus, a tax collector regarded as a sinner (Luke 19:1-10); he entered the home of Levi, where he ate with sinners and tax collectors (Mark 2:13-7); he provided a mysteriously lavish banquet for his hearers where only scarcity appeared to dominate (Matt. 15:32-8). "Now the tax collectors and sinners were all drawing near to him. And the Pharisees and the scribes murmured, saying 'This man receives sinners and eats with them' " (Luke 15:1-2). Jesus is labeled as a "glutton and a drunkard" who eats with sinners (Matt. 11:19).

Somewhere people have gotten the notion that all this eating and drinking just means that Jesus loved to have a good time and enjoyed a good party. Thus, we have the laughing Jesus, the happy-go-lucky Jesus who tells us we should have a good time in life. The point of Jesus' activity, however, is not that he enjoyed a good party. The point is that he restored men and women to their human selfhood through inviting them into intense communal relationships with him and with one another. Jesus offered salvation to those who lived in the kingdom of nonbeing and death through this offer of table-fellowship.

Jesus' meals are parables of God's reign. When God's reign is fully present, all men and women will be united into one community of mutual recognition. No one will be a stranger excluded from the benefits of communion. All people will give and receive the relational acknowledgment that they need in order to know themselves as fully loved children of God. This mutuality and partnership in a common humanity will generate unexpected abundance. The reign of God is a feast, a sumptuous banquet. There will be a time when "many will come from east and west and sit at table with Abraham, Isaac, and Jacob in the kingdom of heaven" (Matt. 8:11).

> When one of those who sat at table with him heard this, he said to him, "Blessed is he who shall eat bread in the kingdom of God!" But he said to him, "A man once gave a great banquet, and invited many; and at the time for the banquet he sent his servant to say to those who had been invited, 'Come; for all is now ready.' But they all alike began to make excuses. The first said to him, 'I have bought a field, and I must go out and see it; I pray you, have me excused.' And another said, 'I have bought five yoke of oxen, and I go to examine them; I pray you, have me excused.' And another said, 'I have married a wife, and therefore I cannot come.' So the servant came and reported this to his master. Then the householder in anger said to his servant, 'Go out quickly to the streets and lanes of the city, and bring in the poor and maimed and blind and lame.' And the servant said, 'Sir, what you commanded has been done, and still there is room.' "
>
> —Luke 14:15-22

Membership and partnership are infinitely expandable. There is always room for more. Indeed, the inclusion of outsiders only increases the resources available for feasting. It can never diminish them.

There is a calculated inefficiency at work in Jesus' hospitality. Those who seem least able, those who appear most as strangers to the dominant social order,

are actually the ones who generate the banquet's rich
provisions and invite others to share in them. Jesus'
parable of the banquet, moreover, criticizes those who
protectively cling to their little circle of like-minded
friends and avoid contact with the public and its
strangers. Those who have assets are reluctant to cross
boundaries that might bring them into contact with
others who are different. They prefer to tend their own
fields and to watch their own oxen rather than to enter
into situations that demand mutual welcomings. They
prefer to stick to the easy and safe intimacy of spouse
and family rather than to welcome strangers at a public
banquet. The truth, however, is that only when men
and women are drawn out of such easy and safe intimacy can they experience the powerful presence of
God's reign.

As Christians, we often like to stay with our intimate
spiritual friends who seldom challenge our basic assumptions. We prefer to plow our own private fields,
never bothering to encounter other spiritual journeyers in congregations and fellowships. Such spiritual assumptions do not produce lavish banquets in
God's reign. Instead, they lead to scarcity and spiritual
starvation. Individualistic assumptions about the spiritual life encourage us to turn away from Jesus' invitation to table-fellowship where we can be drawn into
relationship to him and to others around us.

Jesus' last meal with his disciples must be understood in this same light, as must the prayer for daily
bread. As Jesus' chosen associates, the twelve received
his body and his blood of the covenant. This act en-
abled them to "seal their extraordinary friendship
with him, to take into their very bodies the peace and
trust and hope that they have begun to taste in their
table companionship with him." It drew them into his
continuing work. "After the resurrection it will be-

come clearer to them that they must take up their master's table ministry and become hosts of the kingdom themselves. And they will see that in this task they must also take up a cross, for the restoring of true community always provokes oppression from those who see it as a threat."[9]

The Last Supper serves as a reminder that the means of grace are not the bread and the wine themselves. The real means of grace are the mutuality and the sharing that emerge among those who share a meal with Jesus and with one another. In eating and drinking together, isolated individuals are drawn out of their interior, private lives. With others, they discover themselves as real people who are recognized and affirmed by those around them. When such eating and drinking occurs, Jesus is present. Mutual recognition becomes a means of grace. Is it possible that people stay at home on communion Sundays because they really don't want to be that close to others? To eat and to drink with them in Jesus' company?

There is a kind of sacramentalism that insists the bread and the cup by themselves mediate Christ's presence and grace to us. When we say this, we leave ourselves open to the assumption that we can eat and drink without any recognition of those eating and drinking with us, allowing us to locate the means of grace in the wrong place. Yes, sacramental theology is correct when it insists that the physical can mediate God's grace to us. But the physical reality through which God acts may be the people who share the bread and the cup as much as the bread and cup themselves. To focus too closely upon the bread and cup is to confuse means and ends.

Similarly, there is a misguided rationalism that wants to locate the meaning of the Lord's Supper in the mind of each worshiper. What counts, we often argue, are the pious reflections and religious emotions that the individual can generate within himself or herself. Here too any contact with others around the worshiper is purely incidental and unimportant. Neither view creates a worshiping community. Both create a collection of individuals who relate privately to Jesus but withhold the real means of grace from one another when they refuse to recognize and to affirm one another. I have sat through worship experiences where the ushers moved among the congregation like waiters serving individual meals to private dinner tables. Each worshiper drank from his or her own cup, eating his or her own private crust of bread. I have attended worship experiences where the Lord's Supper was seen as a smorgasbord. The bread and tiny cups were left at the railing and individuals came and went, serving themselves as they wished. When the people refuse to be means of grace to one another, when they ignore one another's presence, when they do not acknowledge or affirm one another, then there can be no other means of grace in the Lord's Supper.

Jesus' healings are also acts through which community is formed and by which isolated, excluded individuals are restored to a community where they can discover their identity. Jesus does more than mend broken bodies and minds. When he welcomes those whose handicaps and disabilities have caused them to be excluded from sociality, Jesus restores them to interpersonal relationships where they can experience themselves as real people. His healings are parables in action. They demonstrate the same truth about God's reign that his table-fellowship does.

Those who suffer from leprosy are not just subject to physical disease and pain. They are also isolated and excluded from the human communities that could affirm and confirm their lives. Those who suffer from various physical deformities or handicaps are not simply physically disfigured; they are also spiritually and psychically wounded. As Erving Goffman has demonstrated in his work on stigmas, the deformed are victims of emotional and social deprivation because they look or act differently. Their differences stigmatize them and isolate them from the routine, everyday social exchanges that most of us depend upon to confirm our identity and sustain our sense of self-worth. "Normal" people do not relate to stigmatized people in the same way that they do to other "normal" people. Victims of such deformities and handicaps are deprived of the means to personal authentication when they are treated in this way. They suffer as much from this deprivation as they do from the physical handicap itself.

The woman with the chronic hemorrhage was not merely physically troubled. She was rendered ritually unclean by her flow of blood. Her "impurity" isolated her from many everyday contacts with others as well as from participation in her religious community. She was excluded from communion through community. When Jesus healed her, he also restored her to human community and communion with others around her. This restoration to communion was the real healing; the physical healing was simply a means to this end. Her salvation came in her restoration to communion and not in her physical healing.

Nowhere is the connection between sin, death, and isolation from communion more evident than in Jesus' healings, in his table-fellowship with sinners, and in his acts of forgiveness.

Most of the stories about Jesus' healing ministry preserved in our Synoptic Gospels highlight the restoration of isolated individuals to communities of loved ones. . . . Thus, the deeper goal of Jesus' healings was to help people recover the mutuality with friends or families that they had lost. This was especially true in the case of those who required the healing of forgiveness, for worst of all about their guilt was the inevitable wall of separation from loving human contact that it had built.[10]

Jesus intended to create a communion where all sorts and conditions of people could find a welcome, where strangers could become partners in recognizing one another's common humanity. Jesus envisioned this mutual welcoming as a lavish feast to which everyone was welcomed by God. We need to remember this not just in our worship and in our celebrations of the Lord's Supper, but also in our church buildings and education facilities. When limited access excludes the elderly or the handicapped from fellowship and from worship, then they are excluded from communion. When our buildings are not means of communion, then it is difficult for the people within the buildings to offer salvation and communion through Jesus to one another.

We have frequently understood sin as moral guilt rather than as a rejection of others, as a turning away from the other person. One consequence of this has been an emphasis upon Jesus' death as a guilt offering, as a sacrifice to atone for our guilt. We have located Jesus primarily upon the cross. We have pictured him at Golgotha with thieves on each side of him and an assortment of unrelated soldiers and onlookers beneath. His community, however, is gone. They stand isolated at a distance, scattered in their solitary hiding places. Christ's redemptive work becomes his sacrificial death upon the cross, something Christ does alone. Its benefits and merits are understood as things each of us claims for ourselves as an answer to our moral guilt. This traditional perspective is almost entirely individualistic. The individual Christian is redeemed privately through his or her relationship to this dying and rising Jesus.[11]

Something important is lost in this picture. The image of Jesus surrounded by those he loved and forgave and opened for communion with him and with each other is missing. Jesus' gospel, his good news, involves restoration to a common humanity. It does not exist as a private contemplation of a distant, isolated God. Jesus' proclamation of God's reign involves a restoration to communion that binds people together as men and women who cannot truly possess a human nature without mutuality and partnership. It is this possibility of communion, of mutuality, of partnership that Jesus restored through his acceptance of his disciples and through his demand that they accept one another. "The miracle that has occurred among us who surround Jesus is that he has loved us and forgiven us and thus reestablished the bond of humanity among us."[12]

Jesus accomplishes our salvation when he establishes the possibility of communion among us. The cross stands primarily as a sign that welcoming the stranger and showing hospitality to other men and women always remains a risk and a threat. Jesus' courageous hospitality toward those caught in a vicious cycle of exclusion and enmity opens up the possibility of human partnerships that can make all people whole persons. It also unleashes the violent hostility of those who benefit from a social economy that excludes and exploits certain individuals and groups.

Jesus overcomes sin and death when he welcomes those who have known only hostile exclusion and have themselves become hostile, violent people.

Sin occurs in a "vicious circle." We sin because we are sinned against, and we are sinned against because we sin. We are indifferent because we meet indifference, and we meet indifference because we are indifferent. Love refused breeds the refusal of love; enmity breeds enmity. . . . The miracle of Jesus is that in him the vicious circle is broken. Here was a man free from the fury of violated humanity, a man who in his faithfulness was able to destroy this fury and to meet the sinner as a man meeting man. Something unheard of was here: a man who would not allow the wrath of the sinner to blind him to the creature who cried from the depths for recognition as creature by his neighbor.[13]

The problem of alienation and the sinfulness of turning our backs on our fellow creatures is surely as serious a problem as our moral guilt. Jesus' spirit continues to be present whenever this vicious cycle of rejection and of death-dealing is broken and overcome. Jesus' spirit manifests itself when men and women face and accept the hostility of those whose humanity has been violated, when men and women still extend a welcoming invitation into communion to those who can accept neither others nor themselves. Such occasions are truly saving moments. In such moments our sinful being-toward-death and our alienating death-dealing toward one another are overcome by life-giving mutual recognition and acceptance into communion.

Notes

1. Haroutunian, 149, 289.
2. John Koenig, *New Testament Hospitality* (Philadelphia: Fortress Press, 1985), 29.

3. Elisabeth Schüssler Fiorenza, *In Memory of Her* (New York: Crossroad,   193),127.
4. Fiorenza, 128.
5. Fiorenza, 128.
6. Theodor H. Gaster, *The Dead Sea Scriptures* (Garden City, N.J.: Doubleday and Company, Anchor Books, 1976), 56-60.
7. Burkhart, 76-7.
8. Linda Weltner, "Nourishment for Stomach, Heart, and Soul," *The Boston Globe* (27 December 1985).
9. Koenig, 41-2.
10. Koenig, 30.
11. Haroutunian, 159.
12. Haroutunian, 160.
13. Haroutunian, 239-40.

FOUR

*Hospitality—Catalyst for Partnerships
in the Gospel*

When the Indian peasant steps into the waters of the Ganges and begins to perform the ancient Hindu rites of ritual cleansing, he or she does so alone. When a man converts to Judaism, he must undergo a ritual washing. He descends into the water and pours it over himself as the rabbi stands above him on the sidelines reciting what a heavy burden he is undertaking by becoming a Jew. The man, please note, must pour the water over himself.

Think for a moment about the last baptism that you observed. Christians do not baptize themselves. It takes more than one person for there to be a baptism. In fact, the person who actually performs the baptism is less significant than the fact that it involves two or more people. In an emergency or a crisis, even the most sacramental traditions allow an ordinary layperson to baptize. The way in which we are made Christians through baptism is itself a sign that Christian faith involves partnership, communion, mutuality.

Baptism is not self-administered but is mediated to us through others. The truth is simple: God's grace comes to us not just through the physical fact of water but also through the mediation of other men and women.

Christian baptizing is something done *to* us. It is not a self-baptism, though we sometimes turn it into one. Christian baptizing "does not involve self-baptism, and the activity of believers recedes completely behind what is done to them."[1] Christian baptism presupposes Christian community. Its locus is not the interior movement of faith within the solitary soul. It is instead the moment of communion between an existing community and a newcomer. Reginald Fuller observes that baptism "brings one into an already existing community. One does not become a believer and then decide to form a society with other believers. Here, perhaps, we can see the importance of the resurrection appearances in relation to baptism. The resurrection appearances created the community. After hearing of the kerygma and faith, baptism is the means by which God inserts new members into the already existing community."[2] The resurrection creates the community of those bound together through being welcomed by Jesus. After that, baptism marks how newcomers are welcomed into this relational, communal partnership in the gospel.

Jesus' saving action restores the possibility of communion where only enmity and alienation had existed. Death had reigned until Jesus Christ. Men and women had withheld from one another the only means by which they could truly recognize themselves and one another as human beings. Jesus Christ saved sinners into humanity by recreating communion between them and himself. He did this by loving them as he loved himself.

For a brief moment after the crucifixion, it appeared

that this communion among men and women in Jesus was ended. The disciples turned on one another, denied one another, fled, or were scattered in solitary hiding places. The resurrection restored the possibility of communion once more. Yet the context of this communion among the disciples was radically changed.

The resurrection has traditionally been seen as a sign of our individual triumph over death. Death somehow cannot destroy our personalities, our souls. Our center of identity is not disintegrated in our physical death. There is, however, another dimension to the resurrection. All the Gospels understand the resurrection as recreating the disciples' communion with one another on a new foundation. The intent of the resurrection appearances seems to have been to reconstitute communion. The appearance of Jesus to Mary Magdalene is instructive. Jesus came to Mary in the garden alone. Yet he refused to let Mary cling individually to him. She was told to rejoin the other disciples (John 20:11-8).

Almost all of the resurrection appearances in John's Gospel involve community. Jesus came and stood in the midst of the community. Resurrection and community were drawn closely together (John 20:19-31; 21:9-14). Even when Jesus appeared to a single disciple, his instructions were always for that person to go join the others. "Do not be afraid; go and tell my brethren to go to Galilee, and there they will see me" (Matt. 28:10). In Luke 14 he joined two disciples as a traveling companion.

Jesus' resurrection appearances were not just demonstrations that he was alive. They were not ends in themselves. Instead, they were a means to the end of constituting a new community of Jesus, the church. This community no longer needed to be bound together by the physical presence of Jesus. Rather, it would be bound together by his spirit.

John's Gospel describes Jesus as attempting to comfort the disciples on the eve of his arrest and crucifixion. He told them not to let their hearts be troubled. He would physically disappear from them but their communion with him and with one another would not thereby be destroyed. Jesus spoke almost entirely in corporate images: household (John 14:2), vine and branches (John 15:1-12), or friendship (John 15:14-5).

While Jesus was alive, the disciples had communion with one another through their communion with him. Now, Jesus teaches them, they would have communion with him only through their communion with one another. Whenever they welcomed and received one another, they would be in communion with him also. "By the church we are to understand an association of human beings saved by Jesus. . . . When Jesus revealed himself as the sinners' neighbor and persuaded them to be neighbors in faithfulness one to another's humanity, he restored community and in that very doing, he founded the church. When a man by the love of Jesus loves his neighbor, there is the church, and nowhere else is the church except in a state of negation and corruption."[3] Jesus consistently taught that the community he gathered together was constituted by relationships and not by hierarchy. So long as Jesus remained physically present to the disciples, the danger of hierarchical dependency was always present. At times Jesus had to confront and correct his disciples on precisely this point (Mark 10:35-45).

After the resurrection, however, the spirit of Jesus can only become present within the community as relational reality. "No longer do I call you servants, for the servant does not know what his master is doing; but I have called you friends, for all that I have heard from my Father I have made known to you" (John 15:15). "I do not pray for these only, but also for those who believe in me through their word, that they may all be one; even as thou, Father, art in me, and I in thee, that they also may be in us, so that the world may believe that thou hast sent me. The glory which thou hast given me I have given to them, that they may be one even as we are one" (John 17:20-2). God has bound our love to God with our love one for another. God insists that we receive our neighbor as the living means of grace both for judgment and for mercy.

The resurrection thus recreates the new community of Jesus as a corporate, relational community. New members enter this community not as individuals who are related privatistically to their God but through the relational dimension of baptism.

A distinguishing characteristic of early Christianity is this positive regard for God's presence in Christ as mediated by community. "What is peculiar to the New Testament is that God is nearer and one's fellowmen are nearer than they are to the Jews and Greeks, the conception of community has quite another importance, the valuations are more intense, and for that reason the emotionally tinged valuating adjectives too are more frequent."[4]

Hospitality becomes a key concept within this relational understanding of the gospel. Churches that hold widely divergent convictions about other matters still seem to value hospitality as a practical virtue and as a Christian conviction. The Letter of James, which derives from early Christianity's Jewish-Christian community, clearly emphasizes hospitality's importance. There must be no favoritism between the rich and poor. The same hospitality is extended to both (James 2:2-4). According to First Timothy 3:2-7, the gift of hospitality must be apparent in those who seek to lead congregations. Love and hospitality are frequently linked. "Above all hold unfailing love for one another, since love covers a multitude of sins. Practice hospitality ungrudgingly to one another" (1 Pet. 4:8-10). The Letter to the Hebrews suggests that in extending hospitality to strangers one is entertaining angels unawares (13:1-2). Paul's letters repeatedly return to this theme. "Let love be genuine; . . . love one another with brotherly affection. . . . Practice hospitality. . . . As for the man who is weak in faith, welcome him, but not for disputes over opinions. . . . Welcome one another, therefore, as Christ has welcomed you, for the glory of God" (Rom. 12:9-10, 13; 14:1; 15:7).

Early Christian missionary communities seem to have worked out the practical implications of such texts. The New Testament alludes to several practices that suggest the conditions behind these texts. Gerd Theissen has suggested that the earliest Christian experience was characterized by homelessness. Christian missionaries were wandering preachers who depended upon the hospitality of others.[5] Congregations were not organized by hierarchical rules of "leaders" and "followers" but by the give-and-take of relationships among friends who each have different gifts. The reign of God breaks into human life when men and women welcome one another as partners.

> Whatever house you enter, first say, "Peace be to this house!" And if a son of peace is there, your peace shall rest upon him; but if not, it shall return to you. And remain in the same house, eating and drinking what they provide, for the laborer deserves his wages; do not go from house to house. Whenever you enter a town and they receive you, eat what is set before you; heal the sick in it and say to them, "The kingdom of God has

come near to you." But whenever you enter a town and they do not receive you, go into its streets and say, "Even the dust of your town that clings to our feet, we wipe off against you; nevertheless know this, that the kingdom of God has come near."

—Luke 10:5-12

God's reign is expressed as coming like an unexpected visitor who is generously received. When a stranger is welcomed, peace and wholeness are established. Even when a guest or visitor is rejected, both parties know that an opportunity has been missed. God has come near even when the wanderer wipes the town's dust from his or her feet.

Paul's letters attest to a tremendous mobility among early Christians. Paul's letter to Rome greets twenty-six people with whom he has had previous contact. Since Paul had not yet been to Rome, he must have encountered these men and women in his other travels. Similarly, they must have been quite mobile to have made their way from the eastern Mediterranean to Rome. Such mobility required practical accommodations and made hospitality and partnership a virtual necessity.

Paul wrote to Philemon with the expectation that a guest room would be prepared for him. Churches were expected to help bear the expenses that a traveler had incurred or would incur. The word *propempo* is used throughout the New Testament with this precise meaning. Titus 3:13-4 employs it to speak of the partnership between congregations and missionaries. Congregations are to help speed Christian travelers on their way by helping with accommodations and expenses. "Do your best to speed Zenas the lawyer and Apollos on their way; see that they lack nothing. And let our people learn to apply themselves to good deeds, so as to help cases of urgent need, and not to be unfruitful."

Paul assumed that local churches would receive him and help to underwrite his travel expenses. Paul told the Corinthians that he would be passing through Macedonia and thus would spend the winter in Corinth (1 Cor. 16:5-8). He wrote to Rome to inform them that he would need housing and assistance there when he passed through on his way to Spain (Rom. 15:23). He also told them that he would first be going through Macedonia on his way to Jerusalem, relying on Macedonian hospitality to assist his journey (Rom. 15:24).

Such hospitality and partnership were not restricted to Paul as the founder and shepherd of these particular churches. Paul claimed the same Christian hospitality for Timothy and for Apollos. "When Timothy comes, see that you put him at ease among you, for he is doing the work of the Lord, as I am. So let no one despise him. Speed him [*propempo*] on his way in peace" (1 Cor. 16:10-1). Nor did such practices end with Paul. If our dating of Third John is roughly accurate, such practices endured in the church well into the second century. "Beloved, it is a loyal thing you do when you render any service to the brethren, especially to strangers, who have testified to your love before the church. You will do well to send them on their journey as befits God's service. . . . So we ought to support such men, that we may be fellow workers in the truth"(3 John 5-6, 8).

Paul's almost obsessive concern with the Jerusalem collection sprung from this same understanding of the church as relational and communal rather than as individual and hierarchical. When Jew and Gentile can bring their different gifts to the Temple and mutually accept and affirm one another, then God's reign will surely come. Paul's interest in the collection was not just to provide welfare payments to the poor Christians who lived in Jerusalem. The Jerusalem collection, Paul hoped, would be a concrete sign of mutual acknowledgment and recognition across a racial and religious boundary. When such differences could be set aside and when mutuality and social acceptance extended, then God's presence would erupt in their midst.

> You will be enriched in every way for great generosity, which through us will produce thanksgiving to God; for the rendering of this service not only supplies the wants of the saints but also overflows in many thanksgivings to God. Under the test of this service, you will glorify God by your obedience in acknowledging the gospel of Christ, and by the generosity of your contribution for them and for all others; while they long for you and pray for you, because of the surpassing grace of God in you.
>
> —2 Corinthians 9:11-4

Paul, however, was never naive about how difficult such mutuality is. Unlike some contemporary advocates of community whose views are tinged by romanticism, Paul was a realist. He understood how difficult such communities are to build and to live within. Community is painful precisely because it is relational. Paul's constant conflict with his opponents in various congregations was one sign of this. Paul understood the conflict and inherent strains of communal life. Parker Palmer also understands: "Once, during a particularly trying time of my life in community, I came up with a definition which still seems true: 'Community is that place where the person you least want to live with always lives!' Later, I developed a corollary: 'And when that person moves away, someone else arises to take his or her place!' "[6]

Nonetheless, the risks were worth it for Paul. He was convinced that hospitality to strangers brought important gifts into the community. Paul's congregations faced death and destruction not when they welcomed strangers as potential partners but when they built barriers to exclude some people or denied the full humanity of others. Sometimes the gifts that strangers brought were hidden behind conflict and congregational controversy. But the gifts were always affirmed. "Travel caused confrontations between Christians of different viewpoints and we are the richer for them because they make us aware of the diversity that characterized early Christianity."[7] It is when we confront those who are different from us and welcome them as potential partners in a common humanity that we are also able to welcome our own repressed and hidden inner strangers as partners in our personal identity. Palmer illuminates this point as well:

> Community always contains the person you least want to live with because there will always be someone who draws out the quality you least like in yourself. The external stranger reminds us of the inner stranger whom we do not want to acknowledge or confront. It is a painful experience, but only as this darkness is "educated" out of us will we be prepared for life together. Such pain is not a denial of community; it is a fulfillment of the role that community can play in our lives, the role of drawing us out into the common life.[8]

Ann Ulanov takes this early Christian insight seriously when she argues that we treat others as foreigners and enemies to the extent that we withhold recognition and acknowledgment from those portions of our own self that we find difficult to accept because they are different or incongruous with our conscious self-image. Welcoming strangers who are different and accepting them, she suggests, is a way to begin recognizing and welcoming those unacceptable parts of our own inner self.[9] Our personal wholeness is predicated upon accepting all parts of our humanness, not just those that fit our self-image. We can take a first step toward this when we begin opening ourselves to those other men and women around us, when we begin recognizing our relatedness to them.

We are saved when the lost parts of our personalities are recognized and lovingly reintegrated into our total self. Until then we are still captive to sin, death, and self-hate. "Any distortion of self, either in degradation or idealization, must be viewed as rejection of actual self and is therefore self-hating. Thus, exaggerated opinions as to one's abilities are self-hating. Minimizing and ignoring one's abilities are no more, no less, self-hating. Rejection of reality as regards self, whatever form it takes, is always self-hating."[10]

Salvation occurs when this self-alienation is overcome. But the patterns of this self-alienation are so deeply hidden within us that they are seldom available to us. What is available and readily accessible are our relationships to others around us. Through welcoming others into our lives, through being drawn out of the safety of our private worlds where we can structure events and people so as to ignore certain parts of our behavior, we open ourselves to the possibility of inner healing.

This is the mistake we make: we think that inner healing and redemption can come only from attention to the inner world of our private experience. In fact, as Ulanov and Palmer suggest, inner healing may arise from outer experience. The interconnections between our interior spiritual journeys and our outward relationships may be more complex and significant than we have often thought. For Paul, at least, holiness and wholeness were intertwined through this exchange between the inward and the outward movements of our lives. Salvation itself depends upon this interplay between inner and outer realities.

Paul had a high understanding of the community of faith and its role in personal salvation. We are saved as individuals, but we are saved through our participation in a community of those who are being saved. How different this is from our usual understanding of the church. How different it is from our usual understanding of why we need to welcome others. For Paul and the early church, hospitality to others was not a practical evangelistic tool. It was essential to the redemptive process itself. Today we speak of "relational evangelism." We seek better ways to incorporate new members because we need their money and their abilities. In doing this, we have turned the early church's ecclesiology upside down and completely reversed the early Christian community's understanding of "private" and "community" life. For us, the church is not a place where through our partnerships in a common humanity we help one another achieve redemption. We do not seek out a congregation that will help us confront unexamined presuppositions and unaccepted dimensions of our personality so that we can integrate these realities into a deeper wholeness/holiness. Instead, we seek the gathering of those who are exactly like us, who will not evoke hidden or buried parts of our personality. We do not seek a place of painful mutual self-discovery. We seek a warm fellowship that confirms our already existing opinions about ourselves.

A couple in the congregation of which I am a part

recently said to me, "I'm not sure we really should keep coming to this church. There just aren't many people like us here." Many people in our society are not seeking a community. They are seeking instead a lifestyle enclave. In a world where we think that we can privately work out our redemption and where we can individualistically define our sense of self, our identity is a product and not a gift. But this identity is always very tentative and fragile. It needs constant affirmation and reinforcement from somewhere, so we seek out others like ourselves to confirm our self-chosen identities. We do not seek communities that are more open and inclusive, because there we might encounter strangers who are different from us. Such strangers would challenge our patterns of self-deception and our partial identities. "Whereas a community attempts to be an inclusive whole, celebrating the interdependence of public and private life and of the different callings of all, lifestyle is fundamentally segmental and celebrates the narcissism of similarity."[11] Perhaps the inability of our congregations to experience genuine moments of personal salvation is intimately related to their inability to see themselves as places of partnership and mutuality. When congregations market themselves as places for the like-minded rather than as places of encounter and communion, then the link between the inner journey and the outer journey is severed.

Our stress upon "fellowship" comes at the expense of genuine partnerships in the gospel. Our emphasis upon congregational intimacy and congregational warmth shortchanges the very difficult interpersonal, relational dynamics that must accompany redemption. Our view of the congregation as a "private" place, as an extension of the family, as a haven from the heartless world, inhibits our ability to offer men and women the salvation and holiness/wholeness that they seek from us.

We need to be much more careful about the metaphors, analogies, and images we use. A church newsletter recently printed a story that encouraged churches to score their effectiveness by the warmth of their welcome. Apparently we really do live by grades and not by grace.

A curious churchman conducted a private survey of 18 churches, which he visited on successive Sundays. He said that he dressed neatly and smiled at folks. He sat near the front and after the service walked slowly to the rear. He remained for coffee when it was served. Then he scored each church on the reception he received as follows:

10 for a smile from another worshiper
10 for a greeting
100 for exchange of names
200 for invitation to coffee or to return
1,000 for introduction to another person
2,000 for invitation to meet the pastor

The researcher reported 11 of 18 churches received scores less than 100. . . . It will be worth it to add up your own score. . . . YOU can make a great difference. Most people come to church because of the fellowship they find and the positive attitude among the people.

Such stories and illustrations are meant to encourage a more hospitable, welcoming attitude among "cold," unfriendly congregations. Yet they also have an unseen, unanticipated, negative impact. Witness the comment of the couple who cannot find anyone "like" them in the congregation. Such illustrations encourage people to look to the church for intimacy, for a place where they can pursue private journeys without confrontation. Do congregations exist to provide warmth and intimacy in a heartless world, or do they exist as a communion in which men and women are means of grace to each other?

Often articles like this are linked to church growth. We should be hospitable and engage in relational evangelism because it will help the church to grow. This seems to be the point behind another article from a church newsletter.

> WAS IT YOU, who spoke to that new person in the parking lot, greeting them cheerfully? . . .
>
> WAS IT YOU, who noticed somebody new seated nearby in worship and offered a genuine welcome with a tip or two about the service? . . .
>
> WAS IT YOU, who invited them to linger after worship in the fellowship time?
>
> WAS IT YOU, who made sure they had a name tag?
>
> WAS IT YOU, who made a point of escorting them to meet the pastor?
>
> WAS IT YOU, who invited them to come to a UMW meeting, join the choir or gave a church pamphlet to them?
>
> WAS IT YOU, who made sure they signed the attendance registration form and even introduced them to the congregation during the appropriate time in worship?

Articles such as this reduce basic, normative values of the early church to purely utilitarian, pragmatic functions. Hospitality to others is regarded simply as a means to church growth.

Such language does not help us realize that our own spiritual journeys are greatly helped by our ability to become companions with others on a common pilgrimage. It obscures the ways in which our spiritual growth is linked to the stranger's spiritual journey. It blinds us to the fact that we are means of grace to one another. Our acts of welcoming have profound implications for our own spiritual journeys as well as for the newcomer's spiritual pilgrimage. "If we deprive ourselves of public experience, we deny ourselves a unique and compelling form of spiritual growth, a unique and compelling sort of communication with God. . . . Without public experience we cannot experience the fullness of God's word for our lives."[12]

Contemporary Christian emphasis upon private religious experience or religious experiences with an intimate circle of friends has tended to turn us in upon ourselves, both as individuals and as congregations. We focus upon our private lives as congregations as much as upon our individually private lives. Thus, we turn our backs to the larger social world in which God is already at work. We avoid dealing with local controversies or public issues because we might disrupt the illusion of a like-minded, intimate fellowship that we foster within our congregational systems.

Recently the congregation of which I am a part has had to deal with two major public controversies. One dealt with offering hospitality to a group of marchers protesting our involvement in Central America and our government's funding of the contra campaign against the Nicarauguan government. The other dealt with an attempt by a railroad to rezone a large tract of land and convert fifty-six acres of woodland into an auto depot transfer station. In both cases, our governing board had difficulty addressing these issues and deciding how to respond. In both cases, the overriding fear was that any action by any part of the congregation would disrupt our warmth and fellowship.

When the preservation of intimacy and fellowship

comes at the expense of helping men and women interpret the meaning of their public lives, then our intimacy has become incestuous. A popular church illustration suggests how this transformation occurs.

A certain man moved into our city. He didn't fall among thieves, he just moved in. By chance, a neighbor came by and saw him. The neighbor said, "I'm running late in my schedule today, and besides, the minister probably knows about him anyway." In like manner, another neighbor came to that place and passing by on the other side, said, "I don't believe in being fanatic about religion. I'll wait until he brings up the subject; then I'll invite him to our church, if he has the time." But a certain neighbor, as he journeyed came where he was, and when he saw him, he was moved with compassion, and stopped by to welcome him and to invite him to church the next Sunday. He even offered to come by for him, which he did. On Sunday morning he turned him over to the minister and said, "Take care of this man for me and whatever else I can do, I'll do it." Now which of these do you think was a good neighbor to him who moved into our city? Go and do thou likewise.

A good neighbor is no longer someone who performs an act of selfless service and affirms our common humanity across hostile barriers. A good neighbor is someone who invites us into interpersonal warmth. In the original parable, the emphasis is upon public life with strangers. In the newsletter version, public life is what one is invited out of. Public life is not where one discovers good neighbors; it is the place one flees in order to find them elsewhere. What was told as a parable about public life in a public place is transformed into a story about private intimacy and warm fellowship.

Is it any wonder, then, that congregations cannot see

any connection between their "spiritual" lives and the church's involvement in social compassion/justice issues? The public life is simply "politics." An expanded understanding of how hospitality and partnership with strangers are spiritual necessities may help change this. If hospitality to strangers is essential to our spiritual journeys, then social justice issues receive an entirely new interpretation. Most issues of social compassion involve welcoming those who are different than we are. They require us to receive strangers as guests and as equals from whom we can learn. They push us toward recognizing oppressed, marginalized people as partners in a common humanity with us. This may mean welcoming the urbanized Hispanic as our partner. The sanctuary movement includes hospitality and partnership across boundaries as essential principles. Hospitality toward and partnership with unborn generations are keys to the whole nuclear arms debate.

Hospitality provides a catalyst for the formation of partnerships among strangers. Such partnerships are essential for our spiritual lives. They are essential if we are truly to discover who we are rather than simply seek confirmation of the self-made identities we have forged for ourselves. They are essential if we are to see God at work in our larger world and know how to connect our work in that world with our own spiritual journeys. They are essential if we are to discover effective ways to welcome new members into our congregations. Our relationships with strangers draw us out of private worlds that can so often deceive and misdirect us. Our partnerships with others in a common humanity shed light upon aspects of our own lives that we may not have seen before. "The viewpoint of the stranger not only affords a fuller look at the outer world; it also gives us a deeper look at ourselves. For the stranger represents possibilities in our own lives which we want to avoid facing. . . . To be comfortable with the external stranger we must be comfortable with that stranger within. But we are not. There are parts of each of us which are poverty-stricken, homeless, hungry for nurture of one kind or another."[13]

God's saving work is not done in the context of our private lives or even in the intimate fellowships that are little more than collections of like-minded individuals. God saves us through our very human, very confusing and often conflicted relationships among a people of God. Such a communion is "a 'priesthood of believers,' doing what they must do as human beings who are bearers of the Spirit of God, approaching one another to give and to receive the humanity for which Christ died and was raised from the dead."[14]

NOTES

1. Ernst Käseman, *Commentary on Romans* (Grand Rapids, MI: Wm. B. Eerdmans, 1978), 164.

2. Reginald H. Fuller, "Christian Initiation in the New Testament," in *Made, Not Born* (Notre Dame: University of Notre Dame Press, 1976), 13.

3. Haroutunian, 234-5.

4. Albert Wifstrand, "Stylistic Problems in the Epistles of James and Peter," in *Studia Theologica* (Lund, Sweden: Prostant Apud C.W.K. Gleerup, 1948), 1:182.

5. Gerd Theissen, *Sociology of Early Palestinian Christianity* (Philadelphia: Fortress Press, 1978), 10-11.

6. Parker J. Palmer, *The Company of Strangers*, (New York: Crossroad, 1981), 124.

7. Abraham J. Malherbe, *Social Aspects of Early Christianity* (Baton Rouge, LA: Louisiana State University Press, 1977), 65.

8. Palmer, *Company of Strangers*, 125.

9. Ann Ulanov, "The Two Strangers," *Union Seminary Quarterly Review* 4 (Summer, 1973), 273-83.

10. Theodore I. Rubin, *Compassion and Self-Hate* (New York: David McKay Company, 1975), 9.

11. Bellah, 72.

12. Palmer, *Company of Strangers*, 56.

13. Palmer, *Company of Strangers*, 66.

14. Haroutunian, 82.

FIVE

*Spirit of the Living God,
Fall Afresh on Us*

Once I asked a neighboring pastor how his congregation was different from the one in which I participate. "The main difference," he said, "is that our congregation is more holy than yours."

"How can you tell that?" I asked.

"That's easy," he continued. "Our people are all Spirit-filled Christians and you don't have the Spirit in your church."

I thanked him for his answer. I even said to him that he might be right. The reasons that I found for the Spirit's absence, however, were very different from the ones that he might give. If the Spirit of the living God is a community gift, then congregations that are collections of private individuals could indeed be said not to possess this Spirit.

There is perhaps no more difficult concept and reality for most of us than the Holy Spirit. Jesus is relatively simple. We can picture him. God, while invisible and unimaginable, can at least be grasped as creator, as "maker of heaven and earth." We may not see God directly; but we can see the handiwork of God the creator all around us. "The heavens are telling the glory of God; and the firmament proclaims his handiwork. Day to day pours forth speech, and night to night declares knowledge" (Psalm 19:1-2).

The Holy Spirit, however, is different. We cannot so easily grasp it, visualize it, fit it into our concepts of reality. And so in our time the experience of the Holy Spirit, which should be a sign of communion and partnership, has become a source of contention and conflict. Some Christians imply their spiritual superiority over others because they possess the Spirit and others do not. Those who have this Spirit sometimes feel that they must gather themselves into like-mind associations apart from other Christians who are presumed not to possess the Spirit.

We have tended to assume that the Spirit is a personal possession—some of us have it and others do not. We have often regarded the Spirit as something outside our normal human equipment and experience. This is slightly curious because we do not make this assumption about God the creator or about Jesus the Christ. Above all, such assumptions have led us to conceive of the Spirit in psychological terms. The movements of the Spirit are something that occur in our psyche. The Spirit is somehow an interior experience.

This assumption has encouraged us to think of the Spirit in private, individual terms. The action of the Holy Spirit, we assume, is something that happens within each of us. It is a private experience. As private and individual, the experience becomes something we can possess, compare with others, or even attempt to manipulate.

"Do you have any Spirit-filled Christians in your church?" the voice over the telephone asked. She was new to town and was looking for a "church-home"—a telling remark in itself. What is a "church-home"? A place of like-mindedness? A place where we will all be alike and not challenge each other's carefully built self-images? More importantly, what is a Spirit-filled Christian? Does the question imply that some people have the Spirit and others do not? Does it imply that some Christians receive the Spirit independently of their communion with other Christians?

What I want to suggest is that the Holy Spirit manifests itself in partnership and in mutuality—in acts of welcoming and hospitality—as well as in solitary, privatized experiences of ecstasy and wonder. This is not the most popular understanding. In fact, it runs counter to most of what we usually mean when we speak of the Holy Spirit. Experiences of the Spirit usually refer to private ecstasies. The Spirit manifests itself in "signs and wonders," in extraordinary demonstrations of power or the supernatural.

In various primitive religions there are shamans who are in touch with the spiritual world and can perform signs and wonders. They possess magical powers through which they can heal the sick, prophesy the future, or cast out evil spirits. The shaman has made a difficult and dangerous ascent into the spiritual world in order to acquire this spiritual power. This power belongs personally to the shaman. It is a private possession.[1] This desire for personal spirit-possession is deeply ingrained in human religiosity.

Our society is fascinated by this individual possession of spiritual power. Perhaps we find it attractive because so many of us feel powerless before impersonal bureaucracies and indifferent institutions. We are seeking individual power, especially private spiritual power. Thus, Carlos Castaneda's books, such as *The Teachings of Don Juan,* have become best-sellers. Such an approach to the life of the Spirit, however, may eventually be self-defeating.

I am constantly amazed by the numbers of former Spirit-filled Christians who have dropped out of all Christian community and have abandoned the Christian faith entirely. They have sought experiences of the Spirit, but eventually those experiences have not led them more deeply into Christian faith. The experiences have instead burned them out on Christian faith. These people have sought individual empowerment in their lives. The promise of the Holy Spirit that will come with power and wonders is very appealing. But when the Spirit does not deliver the expected private gifts, they burn out on Christian faith. They become discouraged and disbelieving because their expectations have not been met.

For many people, the power of the Spirit is the promise of personal power to cope with their individual, private problems and the Spirit is expected to be a private possession. There is some evidence for this possibility. The Hebrew scriptures, in particular, contain examples of this understanding. Samuel and Elijah had great spiritual power and could perform wonders and signs. They had ecstasies themselves and could initiate others into similar ecstasies. After the contest on Mount Carmel, Elijah was so filled with the Spirit that he could outrun the king's chariot (1 Kings 18:46).

We can be led by such traditions and by something deep in the basic religious impulses of humankind to see the Spirit as some sort of interior personal power that we individually possess. When this happens, we are in trouble; we have begun to move in a direction that will eventually sever our lives from the Spirit of the living God, the God of Jesus. The more we see Spirit as a personal possession, the more we separate ourselves from those experiences and communions that can mediate Spirit to us. Thus, we end up like the former Spirit-filled Christians who have been intensely involved in Spirit-filled congregations only to burn out and abandon all attempts at the Christian journey entirely.

There is a short film entitled "The Fable." In it, an actor tells the story of a man who plants a garden. The story unfolds through pantomime; its meaning and impact are so powerful that no words are needed. He plants a garden and, realizing that rabbits and other small animals could eat his plants, sets a fence around the garden. The fence protects the garden from the rabbits, but it is not high enough to keep out larger animals. The next year he builds a bigger wall around it. His yield is abundant. The third year he builds a bigger, higher wall. This time he wants to protect his garden even from the sight of his neighbors. But this time the wall is so high, so solid, so impenetrable, that nothing can grow. The wind, the sunshine, the rain are all blocked out. Everything dies.

The same thing happens with the Holy Spirit. When we begin to see it as a private possession for our benefit, then we begin to create the conditions in which the Spirit dies within us. Spirit is a gift to and of community. It empowers us through connecting us with others. Spirit breaks into our lives when isolation and separation are overcome. In such moments we feel an enhancement of being. We feel that we are suddenly more than we thought we were. Others bestow this gift on us through their acknowledgment and affirmation of us. It is not something that we can do on our own. Empowerment comes through mutual recognition; the energy of the Spirit is connecting energy.

It seems to me that spirit has something to do with the energy of our lives, the life-force that keeps us active and dynamic. . . . Spirit, for me, has a quality of connecting us with each other, with the world around us, and with the mysterious Source of all. . . . Sometimes it seems that will moves easily with the natural flow of spirit, and at such times we feel grounded, centered, and responsive to the needs of the world as they are presented to us. . . . There are other times when will seems to pull away from spirit, trying to chart its own course. This may happen when we feel self-conscious or when we are judging ourselves harshly. . . . At such times, we may feel fragmented, contrived, artificial.[2]

The Pentecostal Spirit fell upon the disciples when they were gathered together with one accord. Their gathering, their communion and mutual partnership were essential to the Spirit's descent.

They returned to Jerusalem from the mount called Olivet, which is near Jerusalem, . . . and when they had entered, they went up to the upper room, where they were staying, Peter and John and James and Andrew, Philip and Thomas, Bartholomew and Matthew, James the son of Alphaeus and Simon the Zealot and Judas the son of James. All these with one accord devoted themselves to prayer, together with the women and Mary the mother of Jesus, and with his brothers.

—Acts 1:12-4

Their first action as a community was to establish new ways of welcoming one another and of receiving outsiders into their midst. They cast lots and then invited Matthias into partnership with them (Acts 1:15–6). Their first action was not a healing. It was not a sign or a wonder. Instead, it was the simple act of welcoming someone into their lives. It was an act of hospitality: welcoming a stranger into relationship and community.

According to Acts, the Spirit did not descend upon the disciples as an individual possession or gift. It came upon them all together. "When the day of Pentecost had come, they were all together in one place" (Acts 2:1). The important sign and wonder was not the tongues of fire but the overcoming of the barriers that prevent community. The barrier of language that had separated men and women since Babel was overcome. They were not separately speaking private languages that only they and God understood. They were speaking in one another's languages. They were speaking so that relationships among separated, isolated peoples could be established. Anyone who has traveled in a country that uses another language knows how frightening it is when no one can understand us. When we cannot make contact with others through language and speech, we feel very isolated. We feel as if we are invisible nonpersons. This isolating aspect of separate languages and cultures was overcome at Pentecost. Acts 2 stands as a reversal of Genesis 11. "At this sound the multitude came together, and they were bewildered, because each one heard them speaking in his own language. And they were amazed and wondered, saying, 'Are not all these who are speaking Galileans? And how is it that we hear, each of us in his own native language?' " (Acts 2:6–8).

While Paul's theology differed in significant ways from that of Luke-Acts, Luke and Paul were in basic agreement that community and Spirit are somehow linked together. Without communion there can be no Spirit. Without Spirit, there can be no communion. For Paul, Spirit erupts into human life when there are transformative partnerships in the gospel. Men and women experience the Spirit's presence and power when they welcome and affirm one another in a community including both friends and strangers. The Holy Spirit appears when strangers acknowledge one another, attend to one another, and establish relationships that create identities in Christ. God's life-giving spirit comes to us in mutuality and in community.

Paul could not conceive of an authentic self apart from participation in some social community. Such a community bestows selfhood upon its members. "It is not permissible to interpret man as an individual, resting within himself and fundamentally separable from the rest of the world. . . . For Paul all God's ways with his creation begin and end in corporeality." Paul believes that "we are always what we are in the mode of belongingness and participation . . . whether in thinking, acting, or suffering."[3] When we cease to belong somewhere, we cease to be human. "For Paul there is no autonomous self, a person wholly free from sovereignty and its obverse, obligation. To be a person is to be in a sphere of influence, to have one's existence shaped by a controlling factor outside the self."[4] We live and move and have our being through our partnerships and our mutuality in community. Only through such partnerships across our differences and divisions can the Holy Spirit bestow its gifts upon us.

Paul's writings return again and again to this theme of hospitality as precondition for the Spirit. Hospitality creates a free and open space in which the Spirit can act among strangers who are becoming partners in a common humanity. Paul's carefully worded and slightly manipulative letter to Philemon urged Onesimus's manumission upon the grounds of Christian hospitality and partnership. In Paul's thinking, the gospel suffered violence when there was not an openness to deeper forms of sharing across boundaries and differences. "Only as believers acknowledge the strangers in their midst and reach out to welcome one another can grace abound for the world."[5] Paul assured Philemon that Philemon's hospitality toward Onesimus would not reduce his own material resources, which surely included other slaves as well as property. Hospitality to Onesimus would actually enrich Philemon, Paul argued.

Hospitality and abundance are closely intertwined. Private searches for abundance are bound to end in frustration and futility. Abundance, both material and spiritual, is a product of community rather than privacy. Community and abundance are as closely linked together as privacy and scarcity. "Formerly he was useless to you, but now he is indeed useful to you and to me. . . . Perhaps this is why he was parted from you for a while, that you might have him back for ever, no longer as a slave but more than a slave, as a beloved brother. . . . So if you consider me your partner, receive him as you would receive me" (Philem. 11, 15–7).

This understanding of Paul's doctrine of the Spirit helps us appreciate his opposition to the Corinthian enthusiasts. Paul's opponents seem to have believed that the Spirit was a private gift, operating within their isolated lives. They understood the Spirit as an interior, psychological experience. Paul, on the other hand, understood it as a social, communal one. The issue of each Christian's particular gift of the Spirit brings this difference into sharper focus.

Paul is careful to avoid the Hellenistic term *pneumatika*. He substitutes instead the term *charism*. The

Holy Spirit is characterized, then, by a relational experience rather than by private experiences that highlight individual differences. Charismata lack the sense of interiority and private superiority present in the term *pneumatika*. "The Spirit which comes from God binds men to Jesus and to his reign," says Hans Kung in his study of the doctrine of the church. Kung goes on to say, "The true charism is not simply a miracle; it is something in the service of the community, giving a sense of responsibility towards the community and the desire to edify and benefit it. . . . Charisms are by no means only exceptional things, they are everyday phenomena in the life of the Church."[6]

The Spirit of God binds people together. It establishes relationships. It enables people to respond to one another. The Spirit acts to make men and women responsible for one another's spiritual well-being, enabling each to share his or her particularity and uniqueness for the enhancement of another's growing wholeness. It enables each to receive, to welcome the other person's different perspective on life into one's own life. "It is not that our view is always wrong and the stranger's always right, but simply that the stranger's view is different, giving us an opportunity to look anew upon familiar things."[7]

The Spirit, community life, and gifts are somehow linked together. We share in the Spirit's life when we receive gifts from others and share our gifts with them in community life. "Gifts of the Spirit come to us when each one is doing just what he or she is called to do, no matter what it is, and no matter whether we know about it."[8]

There is a Hasidic tale based upon the story of Korah's revolt. Korah, a Levite who ministers to the people, becomes jealous of the gifts that Aaron and Moses have and wants to enter the sanctuary like they do. There is a contest between Korah and Aaron and Moses. Moses calls upon God to decide between the two camps. In the judgment, the earth opens up and swallows Korah and his supporters (Num. 16). The Hasidic tale comments: "A disciple asked the rabbi of Kotzk what it was that caused Korah to rebel against Moses and Aaron. 'He had observed' answered the rabbi, 'that whenever he stood up above, among the singing Levites, great gifts of the spirit descended upon him. And so he thought that if he stood within the tabernacle with his censer, still greater gifts would accrue to him. He did not know that the power he had felt came upon him because Aaron stood in his place and he in his.'"[9] Korah assumed that gifts of the Spirit are a private matter; he had his and Aaron had his. Korah's next step was to assume that these private goods could be compared and evaluated as individual properties. Finally, Korah looked at these gifts as discrete items that could be traded, bought, or increased. He forgot that his gift was dependent upon his relationship to Aaron. He mistakenly believed that his gifts were grounded in personal qualities within himself. But our gifts are a matter of our interconnectedness. We receive and can sustain our gifts only because we are present to and responsive to the gifts of others. Korah had his gift only because he and Aaron were in a reciprocal relationship to each other. When he began to see his gift as a private possession to use for his benefit and his benefit alone, he lost not only the gift but his life also.

Paul's opponents were like Korah. They saw only their gift and not their deep dependence upon others within the Christian community. Their gifts made them proudly independent of others rather than helping them to acknowledge their interconnectedness and mutual dependence. Paul's use of the term *koino-*

nia is instructive. We usually translate it as "fellow-ship." We form "koinonia groups," by which we mean small groups of like-minded individuals. Such groups encourage intimacy rather than inclusion. Their object is for people who share quite similar spiritual experiences to support one another. The problem with such groups, however, is that they have no room for greeting the stranger in one another. And without the stranger, growth in the Spirit is difficult. Without the stranger, development of gifts is impaired. "When we meet the stranger, we are engaged in public life, and through such engagement, according to Scripture, gifts of the Spirit will be brought into our lives."[10]

Paul borrowed the word *koinonia* from the language of business and commerce. It is not a term used just for the warm intimacy of family life. It is a public term: "partnership." Koinonia involves a partnership in the common project of proclaiming God's reign. Paul made "a contractual agreement by which members contributed their property, labor, skill . . . toward the achievement of a common goal."[11] Koinonia refers to what in American legal and economic history we would call a public corporation. Each party contributes a "share" and in return receives a "dividend." Paul used *koinonia* in precisely this sense when he referred to his partnership with the Philippians. "You Philippians yourselves know that in the beginning of the gospel, when I left Macedonia, no church entered into partnership [koinonia] with me in giving and receiving except you only; for even in Thessalonica you sent me help once and again" (Phil. 4:15–16). A Spirit-filled congregation, then, is actually one in which men and women who are marked by differences and by individual particularity can give and receive from one another. It is where they can grow together through sharing their own particular gifts and ways of seeing the world with one another.

the Spirit works *among* the believers, in their common life and in their intercourse one with another or others. Even while freedom from anxiety and for love is an individual affair, it, in fact, transpires in the association of human beings called the church. The Spirit of God neither recognizes nor indwells individuals as abstracted from society. His common mode of action requires a living and responsible interaction of people, so much so that there is no working of the Spirit apart from the social life of the church.[12]

Paul's bitter criticism of the Corinthian celebration of the Lord's Supper stemmed from this same understanding of partnerships in the Spirit. The chief sin at such gatherings, Paul claimed, was that believers despised and humiliated one another in just that setting where they should be enhancing one another's worth.[13] Those who had an economic advantage brought ample supplies of food and wine, but they then ate most of this provision before the poor, who had nothing, could arrive. Under such conditions, it was not the "Lord's Supper" that was being eaten. The "Lord's" meal can be celebrated only when there are mutual welcomings across social, economic, and ethnic boundaries. Such a meal serves as an invitation to create hospitable relationships where the possibility of genuine human community, of a common human partnership in the Spirit, is called forth. When the common meal that should affirm the bonds of human community is reduced to a private meal, then there is a demonic spirit present. We are celebrating our "own" meal and not the "Lord's" meal.

Hell can be pictured as a place where such mutuality

is denied. One parable describes hell as a huge banquet hall. Down the center of the room is a long table, ten feet high—so high that no one in the hall can reach the food lavishly piled upon it. Each person has a set of six-foot chopsticks with which to reach the food. The chopsticks, unfortunately, are good only for getting the food from the table. They are not practical for putting it into the mouth. So all people stand with their chopsticks pulling food off the table but dropping it to the floor as they try to manipulate the chopsticks to the mouth. As soon as the food drops to the floor, swarms of dogs gobble it down. The scene is one of frustration, hunger, and despair.

Next, the story goes, one looks into heaven. Heaven has the same huge banquet hall and the same enormous table piled high with food. All the saints have the same six-foot chopsticks. The mood, however, is different. Everyone has plenty to eat. "The saints pick the food off the table, but instead of trying to eat it themselves, they feed one another. Thus no food is lost, and everyone eats very well. And such is the difference between heaven and hell."[14]

The Holy Spirit cannot be present where barriers separate men and women and where people try to pursue their own private gifts of the Spirit without regard for others around them. The Corinthians were even becoming sick and dying because they were not discerning the body of Christ when they celebrated their meals. They were like the men and women with six-foot chopsticks trying to feed only themselves. They had their lavish banquet tables but were starving because they did not discern the body of Christ in one another. They would not feed one another. They refused to welcome one another into their lives, acknowledging their common interdependence.

Churches are not filled with the Spirit when they are

collections of private individuals each pursuing his or her own personal gift. Rather, they are Spirit-filled when they are places of interconnection and mutual partnership. The experience of the Holy Spirit will elude us so long as we try to discern that Spirit apart from our brothers and sisters within the strange world of community life. The demonic spirit will confuse and distort us so long as we, like Korah, forget that our giftedness comes to us through investment, risk, and sharing within gospel partnerships.

Notes

1. Mircea Eliade, *Patterns in Comparative Religion* (New York: New American Library, 1972), 102-6.

2. May, 3.

3. Ernst Käsemann, *Perspectives on Paul* (Philadelphia: Fortress Press, 1971), 17-8, 21.

4. Leander E. Keck, *Paul and His Letters* (Philadelphia: Fortress Press, 1979), 88-9.

5. Koenig, 81.

6. Hans Kung, *The Church* (New York: Sheed and Ward, 1967), 182-3.

7. Palmer, *Company of Strangers*, 58-9.

8. Elaine Prevallet, *Interconnections* (Wallingford, PA: Pendle Hill Pamphlet, 1985), 4.

9. Martin Buber, *Tales of the Hasidim, Later Masters* (New York: Schocken Books, 1948), 274.

10. Palmer, *Company of Strangers*, 57.

11. Koenig, 71-3.

12. Haroutunian, 275.

13. Koenig, 66.

14. Richard W. Chilson, *Prayer Making* (Minneapolis: Winston Press, 1977), 114.

SIX

Pilgrimage into the Strange Absence of God in Public Life

As I stand on the front steps of the church building in which I worship, I can look across the town common and see the steeples of St. Francis Roman Catholic Church and The Congregational Church. Nestled between these two buildings is the senior citizens' center with its congregate feeding program, meals-on-wheels, elder day-care center, and other assorted programs. Just beyond these buildings and up the common slightly is the old town hall where the recreation commission holds its events and programs: aerobics, basketball, babysitting skills classes, and perhaps even an occasional yoga class. Immediately to my left, just next door to the church, are the post office and the bank. This same complex of public buildings includes a medical clinic and outpatient care facility for the nearby hospital. At the north end of the common the police and fire stations guard the town and its residents. At the other end are town offices, business and professional offices, and the town library, where commerce and politics are conducted both publicly and privately.

This is, in many ways, the American myth's typical community. It is picturesque and quaint. What is more striking, however, is the interlocking grid of public institutions. All the major spheres of influence are within sight of one another. As residents do their business with one institution, they are keenly aware of all the others. One cannot pick up mail without being aware of the doctors and nurses coming and going from the clinic. One cannot make a bank deposit without being aware of the church's presence and its judgment upon the dangers of money. Young mothers with infants stroll past the senior center on their way to the local pharmacy.

The various segments of life are not neatly compartmentalized and separated. To touch one institution or organization is to be aware of all the rest. This is the classic pattern of American communities.

> Within the integrated pattern of life in these classic American communities and neighborhoods, people were regularly and frequently in touch with one another—*and so were the primary institutions within which they lived their lives.* Workplace and school building, police and fire stations, grocery store and church building were all within sight of one another. . . . People felt the presence of all of them. . . . In a world composed of such relationships, people also experienced the local church as connected to all of life.[1]

The church's presence pervades all segments of this older community. Even those who are not practicing Christians are aware of the local churches, their imposing steeples, and well-kept lawns. As the church's physical presence links it to all the other local institutions and organizational segments of life, the clergy's

106

presence pervades these same segments of community life. I am known to the local bank officers by name; I am expected to preside or at least be present at a variety of public events, from the installation of the new postmaster to the noon meals at the senior center. This presence penetrates into every town meeting's opening prayer, every high school graduation, and every parade on Memorial Day and Veteran's Day.

Most residents, consciously or unconsciously, depend upon the church's pervasive presence to demonstrate the pervasive presence of God. Similarly, the appearance of some local ordained representative of the church stands as a symbol of God's abiding presence among all these segments of community life. God's providence and prevenience in all parts of our human lives are symbolized by the visible presence of the church and its official representatives in all segments of our lives. "The external pattern of a traditional community, with its interconnectedness and visible presence of the church to all of life, supports a framework that testifies to the Providence of God. Indeed, in such a world, as we have seen, the presence of God seems inescapable."[2]

But my community is changing. Suburban sprawl from nearby metropolitan areas is creeping into the town's open spaces. Farms and woodlands are being bulldozed into housing developments. New residents are moving into town, taxing the school's ability to educate their children, pushing real estate values upward, demanding more and better community services. As population increases, new organizations, clubs, and associations are forming. Newcomers bring with them special interests that generate new groups. This proliferation of groups, organizations, and institutions is itself corrosive to the older interconnections between the town's few, traditional organizations. There simply are too many groups to allow for strong intercommunication and coordination.

Many new residents do not work in the shops, offices, and businesses that are clustered at the end of the common. They commute to the city to work each morning and return exhausted at the day's end. Because they travel out-of-town each day, their business, banking, and medical care may not go on in those traditional places gathered together on the common. The older unity between place of residence and place of employment is broken. This also undermines the old interconnections among the town's traditional institutions.

Life becomes more compartmentalized and segmented. "Daily life, which formerly took place within an integrated community or neighborhood, is now, for most people, composed of separate segments, each isolated from the rest."[3] People who have to hold all these various segments and commitments together experience severe stress. The task of keeping it all together, of balancing the demands of each segment with those of the other segments of one's divided life, of constructing a manageable life requires tremendous emotional energy. Personal identity is not a gift given by one's social roots within a community over time. It is a product that each person must construct on an almost daily basis. "We juggle the multiplicity of demands by carefully scheduling our movements from space to space. We describe our scheduled times as 'commitments,' a powerful word originally used to specify the *overall* boundaries of a person's life. Commitments to various segments are routinely associated with specific times. . . . When living in one segment we feel protected from obligations associated with another."[4] In such a world, the connections between the church and the other segments of one's life are severed. It becomes harder and harder to see the ways in which the church's presence is evident in one's life. Congregations become just one more compartment among all the others. Since the obligations of one segment protect us from those of another, it is harder to see the relevance of the church's traditional ethical and religious values for certain basic parts of one's life. We begin by saying that certain behaviors are appropriate only in certain segments. We learn at school, work at the office, play at the seashore, have faith at church. The next and fateful step is to decide that we are obligated to learn only at school, to work only in the factory, to play only on vacations, to believe in God only in the church. A chasm thus opens between our faith and the rest of our lives. We have depended upon the church's pervasive presence to assure us of God's all-pervasive providence and prevenience. Where the church physically could not go, its official representatives were somehow present. They, as bearers of the institution's holiness, could bring assurance of God's providence and prevenience. But as the church's presence in all segments of our lives is diminished, God's presence in our lives is also diminished. "We can no longer see how God can be effective wherever we can no longer perceive the presence of the church."[5] God, then, is effectively absent from many parts of our daily, public lives.

Such a world poses certain problems for Christian spirituality. When Christian faith becomes only one compartment among all the others in our lives, then something essential is lost from the early Christian vision of human life. Christian faith is no longer a complete way of being human in the world. It is no longer a way to understand what the totality of human existence means as it is lived before God. It can no longer be the "Way" that encompasses all dimensions of human life (Acts 9:2; 19:23; 24:22). Instead, Christian faith is reduced to a set of right beliefs or right actions that one holds only within the confines of the churchly segment of one's life.

People become so accustomed to turning to the church as the place where they live out their faith that they increasingly separate their faith in Christ from the rest of their daily lives and duties. Eventually Christian values and perspectives become so compartmentalized that people lose the ability to see connections between their religious faith and their business ethics, between their Christian values and their leisure-time activities, between Sunday morning and the rest of the week.

Men and women begin to believe that their Christian faith is lived out only within the confines of the churchly compartment. When they go out into other compartments of their lives, the obligations and commitments of those spheres protect them from the obligations and commitments of Christian faith. The older world view that was represented by the New England town common, with all its institutions and organizations clustered around the common, gives way to the image of boxes piled next to one another. The boxes may be adjacent, but they are not connected. They do not open invitingly and hospitably to one another.

Christian faith thus begins to seem irrelevant to the rest of life. "Granted that my Christian faith can offer me peace of heart in the midst of the 'dog-eat-dog' world, but what does it say *to* the world? . . . If Christianity offers peace to us when we 'get away from it all,' does it also say something about the 'it all' that we have got to get back to?"[6] When the church begins to make its peace with such a compartmentalized world, then it is placing itself in a very dangerous spiritual position.

The word religion comes from the Latin roots *re-* (back) and *ligare* (to bind). The concept literally means that which binds back together or ties together; it is a binding together of all that is. Religion is that which integrates, unifies, or makes sense of the whole. Religious faith that settles for less than this is no longer true to its own deepest meaning and purpose.

When we attempt to lead our spiritual lives apart from the nurture, support, and accountability of others, we end up distorting our spiritual growth. The presence of other fellow travelers is essential for our growth. We need companionship and communion with others.

This truth applies as much to congregations as to individuals. Christian congregations dare not settle for being gatherings of the like-minded that are content to be only one compartment of life. Congregations need the companionship of other groups, organizations, and institutions in their communities and neighborhoods. Congregations need to welcome partnerships with other groups and institutions as much as they need to be an inviting place for individuals.

Maybe we can never go back to the older interconnections of the New England town common where it was easy to live out the Christian faith in all compartments of one's life because those compartments were all pervaded by the church's presence. But we dare not settle for being isolated segments that are sealed off from the rest of life. Just as individuals need the support and strength of congregational life if their spiritual journeys are to be healthy, congregations need to seek partnerships and companionable relationships with other groups, organizations, corporations, and institutions in their environment. A congregation that promotes a healthy partnership with such outsiders and strangers will be a congregation that promotes a healthy companionship among its own inner circle of members.

United Methodists in particular should realize this. The word *Connectionalism* has strong historical associations. When one analyzes the Latin root, one discovers that *connection* has the same meaning as religion. It comes from the Latin *com-* (together) and *nectere* (to fasten). A connection is that which fastens together, unifies, integrates. Healthy congregations, congregations that promote the spiritual growth and development of their memberships are congregations where an effort is made to connect the religious dimension with all the other compartments of life. Such congregations strengthen the spiritual lives of members because they encourage the concept of the church as more than a place where one "gets away from it all." They encourage members to connect their Christian faith to all dimensions of their lives just as they encourage their members to seek companionable connections with other Christian journeyers.

Parker Palmer suggests that congregations need to emphasize the public dimension of hospitality as much as the personal need for spiritual friendship and companionship. The church needs to seek out relationships and partnerships with organizational and corporate strangers in the public realm just as faithfully as it seeks to assist individuals in forming spiritual companionships. A one-sided emphasis upon spiritual friendship among individuals can lead to what Palmer calls "salvation by interaction."[7] If individual Christians just share deeply enough, if they just grow intimate enough with one another, then they will all grow in grace. When the spiritual life is reduced to such an ideology of intimacy, it becomes a means of escape rather than a means of grace.

When congregations seek partnerships with other groups, institutions, congregations, and organizations outside themselves, they are modeling an important truth for their members. They are reminding their constituents that Christian faith is not just one compartment of human life. It is something that has implications for all segments of life. The church's partnerships with outside groups and institutions help prevent its members from seeing the church as a compartment sealed off from the rest of life. Such creative partnerships also model on a larger scale what individual Christians are invited to do: extend hospitality to strangers who may be potential partners in the gospel.

There must always be a healthy and creative tension between the congregation's ability to form corporate partnerships with outside groups and its capacity to help its members form strong spiritual bonds with others. A congregation that just emphasizes intimate friendships and supportive spiritual companionships among its members risks becoming ingrown, incestuous, compartmentalized. It promotes a religiosity where Christians are lovers only of themselves rather than lovers of that world for which Christ came and died and rose again. A congregation that just emphasizes partnerships with outside groups in the public realm risks losing its identity.

We need a greater emphasis in our preaching and teaching upon the communal and corporate dimensions of spirituality if we are to reverse our movement toward an overly individualistic piety. But this emphasis must always be held in tension with the church's call to seek out partnerships in the gospel with other groups in the social environment. Without this balance, Christian faith succumbs to an ideology of intimacy, to salvation by interaction. A balance between the need for warm companionship in our spiritual journeys and the need for congregations to seek partnerships with others outside its immediate sphere of influence can give the church the tensile strength necessary to minister on Christ's behalf.

The congregation of which I am a part has struggled to attain this balance. It has not always been a successful struggle or an easy one. We have sought ways to encourage solitary individuals to form spiritual partnerships. We have organized small groups, new classes, and new settings. At the same time we have attempted to extend hospitality to groups in our neighborhood that we usually do not consider church-related.

One weekend during Lent we sponsored a church retreat that sought to deepen our members' communion with one another. Two weeks later, as I discussed in a previous chapter, we opened our building and provided support services to a group of marchers protesting our government's involvement in Central American violence. When our governing board discussed these two events, some members said, "What does a political issue like that have to do with the Christian faith?" Such a response is all too typical in many congregations. It indicates an understanding of the church in the world that sets the church apart as the only place where faith matters. It seeks to seal off the different compartments of life, limiting the purposes and meanings and values of Christian faith to only one compartment.

Hospitality, however, is not just a biblical principle that can guide congregations in ordering and structuring the ways in which their members interact. It is also a theological principle that can direct how congregations govern their relationships to outside groups, organizations, and institutions. We still speak of connectionalism. Yet my experience is that my congregation's life and ministry is pursued in lonely isolation from that of other adjacent congregations in our denomination. When we model such isolation and lack of partnership at the congregational level, how can we possibly communicate the importance of companionship at the personal level? When congregations cannot extend hospitality to other congregations or to outside groups, how can they meaningfully invite their members to open their own personal journeys to spiritual companions?

The Wesleys seemed to understand this truth better than we do. Their understanding of spiritual nurture and transformation envisioned expanding circles of hospitality. It began at the level of two or three individuals who met to share their struggle to become faithful men and women. It fit those intimate spiritual friendships into a scheme of wider corporate partnerships, into a connectional system where groups were drawn out of themselves into the broader community. It ended in a joining of the inner journey with service and partnership in the larger public realm.

A charge to keep I have,
A God to glorify,
A never-dying soul to save,
And fit it for the sky.

To serve the present age,
My calling to fulfill;
O may it all my powers engage
To do my Master's will!

Arm me with jealous care,
As in thy sight to live,
And O thy servant, Lord prepare,
A strict account to give!

Help me to watch and pray,
And on thyself rely,

115

Assured, if I my trust betray,
I shall forever die.[8]

Our Christian pilgrimage involves us in the arduous tasks of watching and praying. Our charge is to glorify God and to fit ourselves for that promised life at God's banquet table. This is a charge we have to keep. It is not accomplished solely by turning inward, by focusing exclusively upon the interior life. Yes, there is a need for solitude and retreat from the busy-ness of our lives. But that solitude and retreat must always be seen against the backdrop of our journeys into the public realm of the present age. Our hospitality must begin with the opening of our spiritual journeys to other friends and companions. But it dare not end there. We must extend a welcoming invitation to the confused and complex world that lies outside the doorstep of our intimate companionships and friendly congregations. When we thus learn to serve the present age we will have also learned how to fit our souls for the sky.

Notes

1. Douglas A. Walrath, *Frameworks* (New York: The Pilgrim Press, 1987), 18–9.

2. Walrath, 66.

3. Walrath, 21.

4. Walrath, 25.

5. Walrath, 66.

6. Richard Mouw, *Called to Worldly Holiness* (Philadelphia: Fortress Press, 1980), 104.

7. Palmer, *Company of Strangers*, 114 and "Borne Again: The Monastic Way to Church Renewal," *Weavings* 1 (Sept. 1986):12–21.

8. Charles Wesley, "A Charge to Keep I Have," in *The Book of Hymns*, no. 150.

About the Author

Thomas R. Hawkins is the pastor of Hope United Methodist Church in Belchertown, Massachusetts. He has previously served other churches in Massachusetts and Indiana. He is also the spiritual director of the Southern New England Walk to Emmaus Movement and is former youth coordinator for the Southern New England Annual Conference.

Mr. Hawkins is the author of *The Potter and the Clay* and *The Unsuspected Power of the Psalms* for Upper Room Books. In addition to his ministry and writing, Mr. Hawkins plays the flute and is an amateur potter.